NO ROYAL ROAD

A Memoir

Julianna C. Adler

Llumina Press

ISBN: 1-932303-89-8 PB
         1-932303-90-1 HC

Printed in the United States of America

Dedicated to:

Sunshine, Pussycat, and Precious,

(alias Christopher, Stephanie, and Nicholas),

and to

Nicole, Eric, Christine

--and *Julianna*

To Christa, my classmate,

Julie Adler

Acknowledgements

Many people encouraged me to write my memoirs, among them a young Disney producer. In 1994, Craig Anderson expressed a genuine interest in my past while filming a segment on my professional activities for the *Walt Disney Salutes the American Teacher* series.

I am very grateful to him, and to Randy, my younger son. After reading the first draft of my work, Randy encouraged me to complete it. "Finish it up foremost for us, your family," he said, "but also for descendants of all the Hungarian refugees of the 1956 revolution against the Russian-supported communist dictatorship whose parents haven't been able to write their own memoirs."

I am thankful to the group of autobiographers who meet on Monday mornings on the Main Line near Philadelphia. Under the skillful guidance of Virginia Strong Newlin, they offer motivation and advice to each other. Without their suggestions, and support, I would not have been able to persevere to the end.

In addition, I consider myself extremely fortunate in having had Virginia accept the responsibility for editing this effort. Her sensitive comments and probing questions allowed me to remember episodes of my early life that might otherwise have remained hidden forever behind the curtain of time.

I am also grateful to my brother, Johnny, for being the brother I loved, admired, and counted on throughout my life and to our parents who protected and nurtured us. In addition, I am indebted to the teachers and friends who influenced my development over the years.

Julianna C. Adler

My heartfelt gratitude is due to graphic artist Mr László Bagi of Philadelphia (www.laszlobagi.com), for his inspired, creative cover page design. I wish to express my thanks to Mr. Francis Laping of Alpha Publications in Blue Bell, PA, for pictures of Budapest after the Revolution, and for the map of Hungary after Trianon.

Last, I have to thank my friend, Don Shore, for having faith in the value of this work, for his constant encouragement, and for standing by me through its completion.

Contents

Prologue

"*Ember tervez, Isten végez* [Man plans, God acts]," says a well-known Hungarian proverb. I had made many plans for my "golden years," but writing my autobiography was not one of them. The project just evolved. To my surprise, recording my past became compelling. The creative process presented me with renewed self-discovery and has made writing an enjoyable, almost daily activity.

My original motivation for this book was to provide my grandchildren with a glimpse into their ancestral heritage. However, looking back, I realize that perhaps in this account of my life there are lessons to be learned by friend and foe alike. I like to think that mine is one of the many life stories that matters, one that succeeded in making a difference. It depicts a life of faith, hope, courage, and survival, a life of successes and failures, of triumphs and defeats. Like so many others, my life was uniquely shaped by twentieth century history. As I recalled events and committed them to paper, I also discovered that the legacy we leave does not have to be monumental to be meaningful.

I believe that this memoir, a description of my early journey through life's trials and tribulations, provides a glimpse into what is required of people in order to survive some of history's darkest hours.

My mother was a well-read, intelligent, thoughtful, and sensitive person. In her search for serenity in the midst of a chaotic life, she frequently quoted from Immanuel Kant: "The three essential ingredients for happiness in life are; Something to Love, Something to Do, and Something to Hope for." (SLSDSH) From early on, I endeavored to live my life in accordance with this principle. I have been fortunate in that I have found these ingredients in abundance along my journey. Now, as I arrive at this final stage, Kant's thoughts continue to provide tranquility to my existence and give meaning to my life. Just how lucky can one get? I have grandchildren to love, my memoirs to write, and eternal life to look forward to.

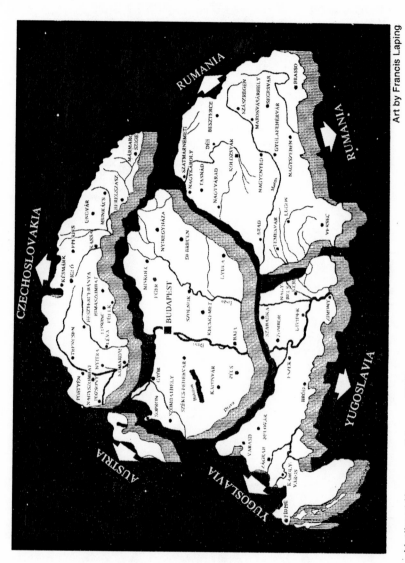

Mutilated Hungary – Trianon, 1920.

Map of Hungary according to the Trianon pact

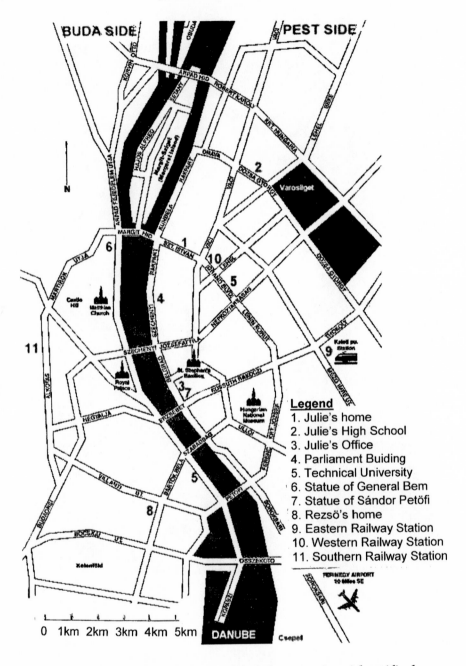

Outline map of Budapest, with relevant sites identified

Chapter One

STARTING OUT

My story starts on the morning of March 17, 1937, in Budapest, Hungary. My father, Zsigmond Adler. a handsome, easygoing, jovial man had taken my pregnant mother, Katalin, to the hospital the day before. They hoped for an uneventful delivery. But night came and nothing happened. The contractions stopped, and still there was no baby. The doctor decided to keep my mother in the hospital because of a slight heart murmur, but sent my father home, reassuring him that nothing was going to happen overnight. Trusting the doctor's judgment, my father spent a quiet evening at home alone — for the last time in his life.

Next morning, well rested, he leisurely made breakfast for himself and cleaned up the kitchen when he was done. He showered, shaved, and spent time combing his unruly, curly black hair, then got dressed in his usual meticulous way, this time in a dark blue pinstriped suit with a vest, shoes and socks to match, white shirt, a solid blue tie, and a matching handkerchief in his lapel pocket. Inspecting his image in the long hallway mirror on his way out, he noted with satisfaction that everything was in place: gold cufflinks, matching tie clip, and his father's antique, gold pocket watch on its chain, one end secured to the lowest buttonhole, peeking out of his left vest pocket. He smiled with satisfaction at the sight of the image of the prosperous businessman he saw in the mirror and slipped his slim, silver cigarette case into the left inner breast pocket and the silver lighter into the right outer pocket of his suit jacket. He picked up a blue hat from the shelf above the mirror as he exited the apartment, carefully locking the door behind.

He proceeded downstairs to call the hospital from the public telephone booth two blocks away from the apartment. When he reached the maternity ward over the telephone and identified himself, an excited voice said, "Oh Mr. Adler, don't worry. Both children and your wife are all right!" As he was later fond of relating, the telephone booth started to spin around, his heart skipped a couple of beats, and his legs collapsed under him. Had the nurse said *children*? "Surely," he said to himself, "there is some mistake. We were expecting one baby, one baby only." In the small apartment there was one crib with one teddy bear in it, one of everything in blue waiting for one new arrival. The word *both* means *two*, he reasoned, so if this is not a mistake, it must be some kind of a joke. By the time he regained his composure, his allotted two minutes were up, the telephone line went dead, and he had no more coins for another call. "Operator, operator," he kept yelling into the handset, but without the required change, the machine just kept staring at him in unsympathetic silence.

He had to walk an additional street block on quiet Pannonia Street before reaching busy St. Stephens Ring Road, where he bought two bouquets of violets from a street vendor before hailing a taxi. The twenty-minute ride through the cobblestone streets of Budapest to the hospital seemed to take forever. Conflicting emotions and thoughts raced around my father's head as the taxi slowly made its way along the busy streets. The worsening political climate in Europe and its possible consequences to his life were never far from his thoughts. "Don't people realize that there is a war coming?" he asked the taxi driver. "How can they not be afraid of what tomorrow will bring?" "Everybody is afraid," the driver replied with genuine conviction in his voice, "but you learn to master your fears for the sake of the children.

They make our struggles worthwhile." "I, too, have a family now," my father thought to himself proudly, wondering if he had two boys, two girls, or one of each, and praying fervently that whatever they were, they would be healthy.

When my parents had decided to start a family, my father's overwhelming desire to have a child had overcome his uneasiness about the political climate in Europe, particularly in Hitler's Germany. Since both my parents were of Jewish descent, they followed the stories circulating about the persecution of people of that religion with increasing alarm. My father could not help but be pessimistic about current events. In a stable world, he knew he could provide for his family, but, given the political climate, he was filled with apprehension about the future of Hungary and his own ability to raise a child under these adverse conditions.

Although the knowledge that he had two children now added to his anxiety, being the eternal optimist he was, he looked at them as a special gift from God, a sign of His trust. It made him realize that he had to succeed in seeing them grow up regardless of the world, that there was no turning back now. His resolve and his pride in his new family energized his every step as he quickly climbed the stairs to the maternity ward.

The obstetrician greeted him with a mischievous smile on his face and started reciting the well-known nursery rhyme, "Jack and Jill went up the hill to fetch a pail of water, Jack fell down and broke his crown and Jill came tumbling after." Then he continued in a more serious vein.

"Early this morning, your wife gave birth to a little boy who weighed in at three pounds, eight ounces, and half an hour later to a little girl, three pounds, four ounces. The reason we could not tell before that your wife was carrying more than one baby is because the children were lying on top of each other and we heard only one heartbeat."

The pediatrician, who was also present, said, "Right now, the bad news is that both infants are tiny, but the good news is that, being full-term babies, they appear to be strong and healthy. Don't worry, for despite their small size, the chances are good that they will survive and thrive since they are fully developed."

Overwhelmed by love, my parents were not particularly worried. To them, we both looked beautiful and perfect, even the tiny girl being taken home from the hospital dressed in blue like her brother.

With the help of good friends and kindhearted strangers, my parents battled to ensure our survival. My mother didn't have enough milk for both of us, so for months we lived on donated breast milk, which had to be ferried by volunteer messengers three times a day by foot, bus, or tram, and sometimes, as a last resort, by taxi. The operation must have taken some logistics at that time, with none of the modern conveniences available that we take for granted today. My parents didn't have a telephone in the apartment and there were no refrigerators in those days. Was it due to sheer luck, our parents' devotion, or perhaps a benevolent God that we didn't starve to death, but managed to survive, even thrive?

My parents named my brother János (John) and me, Julianna, as the Hungarian equivalents of Hansel and Gretel. According to the Hungarian version of the story, it is Jancsi (János) and Juliska (Julianna) who survive poverty and hunger to cleverly outwit the wicked witch of the forest, resulting in the triumph of good over evil.

Chapter Two

BEFORE THE STORM

My mother, Katalin (Katie), was twenty-three years old and my father, Zsigmond (Sigismund), thirty-seven when we were born. They had been married three years earlier, on May 15, 1934, a bright, sunny spring day, by a rabbi in a formal ceremony and surrounded by friends and relatives. My mother wore a long, white lace gown that accentuated her slim body. As she walked down the aisle, a lace veil covering her mid-length auburn hair cascaded down her back to the floor, framing her high forehead, expressive hazel eyes, and fine features. Her radiant smile revealed beautiful, strong, pearly white teeth and charmed everybody. Waiting by the canopy, my father looked dashing in his black suit, which outlined a lean, muscular body crowned by a gracious face with an ever-smiling, friendly expression. He loved to recall later how tears of happiness filled his eyes at the sight of his bride.

By coincidence, my mother's maiden name was Adler, even though my parents were not related to each other by bloodlines. She liked to remark jokingly that the only reason she married my father was because she didn't have to take on a new surname. My parents were very different, but they complemented each other well, and my father adored and spoiled my mother all her life. She was beautiful, but fragile and somewhat shy, while, in addition to being handsome, my father was a popular, active sportsman, an excellent soccer player with many friends.

My father was born in Budapest, while my mother was an orphan, from Pozsony, a provincial town in northeastern Hungary (now part of Slovakia). Her mother, Hermina, died of an undisclosed illness when my mother was just seven years old, and her father, a waiter, died young from alcohol-related causes when my mother was fourteen. My mother and her younger sister, Dusi, continued to live, virtually by themselves, in a small room adjacent to their maternal grandparents' home. Mother was a smart, ambitious woman who earned a high school diploma by the time she was eighteen, a great distinction for a young girl in her time. After graduating, she worked as a book-keeper to support herself, both before and during the early years of their marriage and then again in later life when the extra income was sorely needed to help provide for the family.

As a consequence of being involved in a love triangle, my mother's younger sister, Dusi, committed suicide in her late teens. Apparently she was in love with two men, both of whom pressured her for marriage. She was torn between the two and distraught over the inevitability of hurting one of them. In a moment of despair, she lost sight of the fact that by ending her own life she would hurt both men in addition to many other people. Losing her sister was extremely hard on my mother, especially since she was the one who found her hanging from the rafters in the attic of their home.

Later my mother became close to her two cousins: popular, lovely Aunt Eva and high-spirited Aunt Ika. But of course, neither of them could take the place of her beloved sister. The cousins both married into wealth, although their good fortune was short-lived, for they lost their first husbands during the Second World War. Both of them also remarried. Aunt Eva married a doctor, while Aunt Ika married a communist functionary, a high-ranking bureaucrat in the interior ministry. Both women had daughters from their first marriages. Aunt Eva's daughter, Andy, was born in 1939, and Aunt Ika's daughter, Zita, in 1940.

After the war, Aunt Eva worked in her husband's medical office, while Aunt Ika did some clerical work at the interior ministry. Except for the war years, both of my mother's cousins led a relatively comfortable existence, thanks largely to their second husbands' stations in life. Under the communist, state-sponsored medical system, being a doctor was a lucrative business. Uncle Gyuri, Aunt Eva's husband, did well, even though salaries paid by the state were low. To compensate for the low salaries, patients ended up bringing gifts to their doctors, or paying in order to get good service and extra medicine. Of course, since Uncle Sándor, Aunt Ika's husband, was a Communist Party member with a good salary and connections, he was able to arrange for special privileges for the family, like vacations and shopping trips to state stores stocked with western merchandise. Despite their material comforts, however, both women reportedly led unhappy lives in unhappy second marriages.

My father was the elder of two sons born to parents of modest, working-class backgrounds. My paternal grandfather, Ferenc (Franz), was a skilled typographer with a printing and publishing company, and my grandmother, Anna, was a housewife. I remember visiting their small, dark apartment on the ground floor of a huge stone building across a courtyard lined with rocks. I could not have been more than three or four years old at the time. I have a picture in my mind of my grandfather raising me in the air as he laughingly rubbed his mustache against my face to get me to squeal in protest. I also remember sitting in my grandmother's lap and being warm and cozy as she cuddled me in her arms. She was a big woman with a warm smile and wavy gray hair twisted into a bun at the back of her head. I wish we could have had more time together. They died during the early years of the war, when I was still little, and thus I missed out on their love.

Uncle Nándi, my father's younger brother, his wife, Aunt Manci, and their daughter, Eva (who is a year younger than I am), lived on the second floor in the same building as my grandparents. I don't remember how Uncle Nándi made his living, but stories abound about his happy-go-lucky character, his easygoing lifestyle, and his drinking, smoking and partying. He died in a Nazi concentration camp during the war. The story has it that he gave up his last piece of bread for a cigarette, sat down in a ditch by the roadside puffing away on it, and was shot dead by a German guard when he refused to move. Aunt Manci never remarried. She was a skilled, much-sought-after dressmaker who dedicated herself to her daughter, the loving memory of her deceased husband, and her work.

At age fourteen, my father started working as a stock boy for a store specializing in the sale of fabrics and notions to tailors and dressmakers. Through the years, he worked his way up to be a highly respected sales associate and buyer. He was a clever, hardworking, frugal man who hoped eventually to open his own store in partnership with a friend we called Uncle Jóska, and so he did. Uncle Jóska provided most of the capital, while my father supplied the expertise—and most of the work—and my mother kept the books. The store started out small, but it was in an excellent location on fashionable Váci Street in the heart of Budapest. Knowing that they would get quality service and merchandise at reasonable prices in his new establishment, many longtime customers followed my father from the old store to his new business.

My father loved every aspect of his new life. He loved waiting on customers, rearranging the many reams of fabrics on the shelves, decorating and redecorating the store, and displaying his latest acquisitions in the small window facing the street. People would stop to admire his artistic, imaginative window displays and in no time find themselves inside the store discussing topics ranging from the latest fashion trends to sports, family, and the state of the world. If they left without buying, that was fine with my father. "They will be back," he would cheerfully predict, and usually they were, sometimes with friends in tow. For my parents, the store was a dream come true, however short-lived that dream turned out to be.

I loved being taken to the store by my mother for occasional visits. I loved to watch my father make a sale, the way he carefully counted, measured, and cut the merchandise, the meticulous way he would fold and wrap those fine materials before handing them to the customer. When I was behaving as a good little girl should, he would let me "help" with arranging the store display or with sorting and counting notions. He had me counting those snaps and buttons, adding and subtracting them all the time, for I liked doing it, and he noticed that I was good at it. "Some day you will be a good bookkeeper like your mother, or who knows, maybe a famous mathematician," he would say with unmistakable pride in his voice. He showed me how to wrap things so the corners were sharp, the paper was smooth and the folds were straight. "If it is worth doing, it is worth doing well," he would admonish me each time I thought my work was good enough (but he didn't) until I earned his praise for a job well done. I was especially delighted when on occasion he would call me *kis okos,* an endearing Hungarian name meaning "little clever one," his ultimate praise for me.

I must have been only four or five years old at the time, which makes me wonder if my life-long desire for excellence is due to these early experiences, or perhaps to some kind of genetic disposition I inherited from my father. Most likely, a burning desire to excel, like so many other traits, results from a combination of nature and nurture. In any case, I have my parents to thank for what I consider to be a valuable standard that helped shape my life.

Among the many important influences that contribute to the development of young children is the cultural, historical, and physical environment of their native city. Like Paris, London, or Rome, Budapest is a vibrant metropolis. Lying in central Europe, it is shaped by its rivers and the many bridges spanning their banks. I can still close my eyes and transport myself back to its streets and parks. I can see the sights, hear the sounds, and smell the aroma of this great city where I grew up. In my mind, I can visit the museums with their vast collection of artwork, listen to the masters in the magnificent opera house, attend the many theaters, and, of course, browse the splendid pastry shops, most notably the venerable Café Gerbaud on Vörösmarty Square.

The historic city of Budapest straddles the Danube River, with Buda on the hilly western side and Pest on the flat eastern side. We lived on the Pest side in a nice little two-room apartment on Pannonia Street off the central ring road in a middle-class neighborhood not far from downtown and near the Danube River and Margaret Island.

The apartment house, a large stone building, was located on a street corner with about thirty apartments on five floors, most of them facing a street. Our windows faced the large inner central courtyard, which was considered to be a less desirable location, but had the advantage of providing an excellent view of the open corridor bordered by wrought iron railings, leading to most of the apartments. We lived on the third floor, so sitting at my window, daydreaming, I could see a patch of sky above and had a grand view of the comings and goings of many of our neighbors.

At the entrance of our apartment was a relatively large vestibule, with the kitchen on the right and a long hallway to the left, leading to a bathroom with a tub and a washbasin, and a toilet room called the "WC" along the right side. I only learned the exact meaning of "WC" (water closet) when I visited England about forty years later. At the far end of the hallway, my parents occupied the larger room, which during the day served as the living room for the family, while my brother and I had the smaller room opening from theirs, opposite to the hall entrance. During the day, the radio in my parents' room by the window was always turned on and usually tuned to classical music. Our home was nice, always clean, neat, comfortable, warm, and homey.

On entering the apartment building from the street through a large ornate door into a spacious foyer and ascending a few stairs, you found yourself at the bottom of an imposing enclosed staircase, with the stairs winding around the open sided, wrought-iron fenced, elevator shaft. The landing on each floor opened through a double swinging door paneled with frosted glass. This door led to the central galleries around the courtyard.

My father used to make me count all those stairs leading up to our apartment, coming and going. Eight steps up from the foyer to the first landing, then six more in the stairwell to reach the elevator on the ground floor. All together, fourteen steps, right? That was very easy to understand. It took twenty-one steps to mount to each floor, so, "How many steps for two, three, even ten floors?" he would ask. "How many jumps if you take the stairs by twos or threes?" I always participated eagerly, hoping for the praise, *kis okos*, rewarding my successful efforts. We skipped and jumped and danced like Shirley Temple and Bojangles; he made a great game out of it. He called me Curly Top, for I had short, naturally curly hair, just like Shirley Temple. My father loved to come up with games that involved numbers and I loved playing along, while my brother would simply race up the stairs, or down, being interested only in who was first or who climbed the most stairs. My mother always took the small elevator, never the stairs, so as not to strain her heart. When we went out with her, the aim of the game was to be faster and arrive on the landings before my mother stepped out of the elevator.

As long as I can remember, we had Auntie Mariska as a housekeeper. Since my mother was in poor health due to her weak heart, she needed help with household chores. Auntie Mariska was a middle-aged spinster, with no family of her own, from a small peasant village in the eastern plains of Hungary. She looked, dressed, and acted the part of a housekeeper. A scarf always covered her light brown, braided hair, and she wore a white blouse or sweater and a dark skirt always topped by a clean apron. A devout Catholic, she went to church every Sunday morning and on religious holidays. She seemed at peace with her lot in life and found great satisfaction in cooking and cleaning for us. Over the years, she became our surrogate grandmother and stood by us in good times and bad, dispensing her down-to-earth advice (mostly unsolicited) on life in general, and on special events in particular. She resided in a small alcove (just big enough for a bed) off the entrance hallway to the apartment, with a wooden and stained glass divider for privacy. However, she ruled the kitchen, and justly so. She was a fabulous cook whose pastries were renowned. Rumor had it that she had plenty of offers over the years for better positions, but she couldn't part with her twins, her adopted family. She tirelessly cleaned up after us, kept us in spotless, freshly pressed outfits, and cooked our favorite meals.

My brother, Johnny (or Janika, as she liked to call him), was the apple of her eye, and over the years it became evident to everybody that she took extra care to please him in any way she could. She did not dislike me; she just thought he was more special and did not hide her sentiment. She would cook his favorite meals, bake his favorite cookies, and give him extra candy and chocolates at every opportunity. I often wonder, now, how much of Auntie Mariska's preferential treatment of Johnny influenced my belief that my parents also favored my brother, a belief that haunted me for years. Not that it matters any more, for I know now that both my mother and my father loved me for who they thought I was and over the years did their best by me.

Despite our affection for each other, Johnny and I fought a lot when we were growing up. Even though we are twins, we are quite different in appearance and personality. Since we are fraternal twins, we come from two different eggs and, of course, two different sperm cells. I was told that I resemble my mother's side of the family, while my brother seems to resemble my father's side. Except for my curly hair, which I must have inherited from my father, I look more like my mother, with her light complexion, eyes, smile, and figure. I was a chubby little girl till my teens; while my brother was always lean, muscular, and agile like my father. He also has my father's light olive complexion, black hair, warm, friendly eyes, and smile. Many times, when my cousin, Eva (my father's brother's daughter), who also has an olive complexion, a lean figure, and expressive dark eyes, went somewhere with us, people who didn't know us would think that Eva and Johnny were the twins and I was the cousin. (Though Johnny and I have lived completely separate lives, today people tell us that we resemble each other and have many of the same traits and mannerisms. And, by now, the years have washed away most of our disagreements—the jealousies, the petty resentments—leaving a feeling of genuine camaraderie and a sincere appreciation and love between us.)

We lived about five city blocks from St Stephen's park, on the banks of the Danube River, which had a nice large playground. Every morning, my mother or Auntie Mariska would take us for a walk or to the park, where we played with children of our age. Occasionally we would ride our tricycles or build castles in the sandbox. The girls would play with dolls or play hopscotch endlessly, while the boys chased around after soccer balls.

I seldom took my doll, Katie, along; she was too special for me to share with anyone outside my home. She resembled a two to three-year-old girl scaled down to about eighteen inches and was made of soft flesh-like synthetic material, with arms and legs that moved and beautiful blue eyes with lashes that closed and opened when she was laid down or placed in an upright position. She was so realistic, down to her little toenails, that it wasn't hard for me to endow her with human characteristics. Auntie Maria, a friend of my parents, made a beautiful wardrobe for her, complete with a nightgown that had a delicate white crocheted lace collar and a matching lace nightcap and booties. Katie went to bed in style every night, covered by an exquisite little afghan, also handmade by Auntie Maria, an elderly lady with severe arthritis who had to walk with a cane. Her hands were noticeably deformed, but, despite this, she constantly knitted and crocheted, producing remarkably artistic accessories that she sold or gave away as presents. One of her masterpieces, a large intricately crocheted table cover, that she gave my parents after the war, adorns my dining room table to this day.

My mother loved to knit too, but it was Auntie Maria, who in my early childhood patiently taught me how to knit and crochet, an art that has enriched my life.

On weekends or special occasions, we didn't go to the park, but to beautiful Margaret Island for a walk with our parents, either by a roundabout way crossing Margaret Bridge or by ferry. Going by ferry was a special treat for two reasons. First, we did not have to walk around and across the bridge before we got to interesting destinations on the island, like the large playground, the public pools, or the restaurant with its magnificent pastry shop. (Sometimes on Sunday afternoons we would visit the bandstand, where we could listen to free concerts while having a picnic on the grass. When the adults were not paying attention, we would sneak lemon wedges from the iced tea and lick them in front of the wind players of the band. We thought it was great fun to watch as they struggled to play their instruments despite the natural juices flooding their mouths. Of course, during intermission we were always chased away and reprimanded.)

Second, and best of all, was the boat ride. Through the ferry's small windows we could look below the deck at the steam engine with its shiny pistons and watch the men shovel coal through a small door into the fiery belly of the boiler. I felt sorry for them, for they were sweaty and dirty, as they worked doggedly in the dark hull. Occasionally, the captain of the boat allowed us to climb the stairs to the pilothouse on a platform, located in front of the chimney above the deck, which housed the large wheel and some instruments. Looking out the windows, we could watch him steer the boat across the river and dock at the pier. When the captain was in a really good mood, he would lift one of us in his arms, so we could pull a steel cable that allowed steam to escape through a small pipe, which blew the horn before the boat's departure. I loved standing at the bow, watching the waves go by and dreaming of taking a boat ride up the Danube River to Vienna and beyond, perhaps one day even crossing the ocean.

Occasionally, instead of going to the park or the island, Auntie Mariska would take us to the nearby western railway station to watch the trains come and go. The building was enormous, an architectural wonder at the time of its completion. I always found it exciting to watch the trains and the people. We would walk up to the magnificent black steam engine, with the coal tender attached, at the front of the train and watch the engineers prepare for departure. Two men had to fire up the engine by shoveling coal into the fiery boiler through small doors, while the chief engineer kept checking dials and valves on a panel above. When the gigantic wheels started to turn, slowly pulling the train, I could not help wishing that I could be on it, preferably in one of the first-class compartments, heading for adventure in some faraway land.

At age five, Johnny and I started kindergarten three times a week. We knew many of our classmates and fitted in well with the activities, most of them being organized play, painting, and singing little songs. Most of what we were expected to learn, we knew already, but I participated obediently and did everything I was asked to please the teacher and my parents (and for a good grade or remark on my report card). Johnny was different. He was bored most of the time and frequently got into all kinds of mischief. He liked to play with mechanical toys like trains, cars, and erector sets, and he did not like to share, especially parts he needed for his creations. His reports were far from glowing, but most of his bad behavior was forgiven, for Johnny was bright, and cute, and he discovered early on how to turn on charm to get his way and to keep himself out of serious trouble.

We had many board games at home. Early in life we learned to play chess, nine man morris, tic-tac-toe, dominoes, and we constantly pestered every available adult to play with us. Sometimes my brother and I played these games with each other. However, our games inevitably ended in a fierce dispute, with the losing party accusing the winning one of cheating.

Uncle Jóska, my father's friend, didn't have any children of his own, so he often visited just to play with us. He was a tall, strong, muscular, middle-aged man with most amazing, thick, white hair above his expressive, handsome face. He had a great sense of humor, loved the theater, and appreciated classical music and good jazz. According to the prevailing attitude of the time, girls were supposed to play with dolls, which I did at times, with my one and only, beloved, darling Katie doll. The general consensus was that girls couldn't play mind games well. However, if that is what Uncle Jóska was thinking, he never showed it. He always made time for playing games with me during his visits and patiently provided me with additional challenges to overcome. I was an industrious pupil, and practicing to be a good chess player was fun for me. "You have a good head on your shoulders. You are becoming quite a thinker—especially for a girl," he would tease me. At this point, praise did not matter to me. I had a single-minded goal: to become a good enough chess player to beat my "brilliant" brother consistently. I guess the often-repeated assumption that haunted me most of my early life, that "Johnny is smart, but Julie works hard," had its seeds planted around this time.

Occasionally friends of my parents who had children visited. While the adults played cards and discussed politics in hushed tones, we children played with the many toys we had. Birthday parties were particularly fun. That was when we were allowed to eat all the cakes and drink all the chocolate milk we wanted, not to mention the gifts we received,

I especially liked it when my parents got together with the Marcali family, one of my mother's good friends, for I really liked their only son, Viktor, who was a year older than we were. He was cute and always cheerful, with a twinkle in his eyes, and he made me laugh. He played the piano well by ear, but he also took lessons and practiced diligently from a very early age. I could tell that he liked me too. One day he told me that he liked smart girls, that he thought I was one of them, and that he considered me the sister he never had. Our friendship continued well into our teens, with occasional meetings when we discussed earnestly our problems, our trials and tribulations, and our hopes for the future.

It was around this time, I believe, that I saw my first Walt Disney movie, *Pinocchio;* soon followed by *Bambi, Snow White,* and *Cinderella.* I enjoyed the stories and the music, and I allowed them to carry me away into a magical, colorful, fantasy world, where scary things happened, but where good always triumphed over evil.

Just as Disney films were very special for me, so was Christmas, a holiday I have looked forward to all my life with excitement and anticipation. When we were little, we were told that Christmas was the birthday of the child Jesus, who would send his angels to reward good little children with a Christmas tree, toys, and candy, while bad children would get only a bag of coal and tree twigs. The bad child would have to kneel on the coal in the corner of the room until, with gentle prodding from his parents, he realized the mistakes that led to his bad behavior, and the twigs and tree branches were to be used for spanking in case he didn't see his mistakes. The choice was obvious, of course, and by the time Christmas rolled around, there were only good children in every household. In Hungary, Santa Claus has his own feast day, December 5th (which is also my mother's birthday and the anniversary of her death), when good children receive chocolate and candy, while bad ones get coal and tree twigs as a forewarning to mend their ways by Christmas.

During the afternoon of Christmas Eve, Johnny and I would be taken for a visit with friends by my mother, which allowed time for my father to set up the tree and presents without us nosing around. We would come home to find a beautifully set dinner table in our parents' room, and the door to the children's room would be closed. We could hardly contain our excitement during dinner, as we imagined the angels in our room putting up the tree and the presents. We were always on our best behavior, just to make sure.

Auntie Mariska always made a special dinner for Christmas Eve that started with a cold egg casserole _(kaszinótojás)_ for the appetizer, next came fish soup made with the head, tail, eggs and milk of carp _(Halászlé)_, and then fried, breaded carp slices garnished with potato salad. This festive meal ended with the Christmas pastries _(diós és mákos beigli)_ that had walnut and poppy seed fillings. She had been baking for days.

At the sound of bells, we were excused from the table and the door was opened to reveal the beautiful large tree glistening in front of the window, with shiny ornaments and shimmering real candles. The tree was laden with Christmas candy _(szaloncukor)_ wrapped in foil paper, and all the toys lay beneath its branches. That's how I met my beautiful Katie doll. One year, she was sitting under the tree, waiting for me. She was not much smaller than I was at the time. On Christmas Eve, we were allowed to stay up and play as long as we were able to, with our mother and father joining in the festivities.

By the time we were six years old, the war was approaching Hungary's doorsteps, but my parents shielded us as long as they could from the realization that something was amiss in the world around us. Thanks to their efforts, the early years of our lives were good. Unaware of the storm brewing around us, we were nurtured in a loving, peaceful environment.

Chapter Three

THE TEMPEST

After the conclusion of the First World War and under the terms of the Treaty of Trianon in 1920, because Hungary was on the losing side, it was dispossessed of two-thirds of its territory and three-fifths of its population. In the 1930s, therefore, Hungary's leadership looked to Germany and Italy for a border revision that would remedy these injustices. Meanwhile, social and economic upheaval in Germany resulted in the ascent to power in 1933 of Hitler and the Nazi party.

As a result of the political situation in Europe, Hungary aligned herself with Nazi Germany and was governed by the right-wing dictatorship of Admiral Miklós Horthy. When Hitler's Germany attacked the Soviet Union in June 1941, Hungary also declared war against the Western Allies. Parts of the Hungarian army joined forces with the German invasion forces on the eastern front, while the rest remained in the country to support the dictatorship. In 1943, as the Soviet army pushed the invaders back from the east towards Budapest, the Germans decided to occupy Hungary and installed an extreme fascist government. This move resulted in the introduction of anti-Jewish legislation and an increased persecution of the Jews, first in the countryside, then in June of 1944 in Budapest. During that period, many Jews were taken to Auschwitz or lined up along the riverbanks and shot. They fell into the Danube coloring the river red.

In the spring of 1942, my father was conscripted into the labor battalion, a branch of the Hungarian army made up of men of minorities, such as gypsies, and Jews. These conscripts were used as forced laborers in support of the regular army — clearing roads, building fortifications — under the ever-watchful eyes of armed guards. Fortunately, because of his background, my father was selected to work as a tailor, repairing uniforms for the unit he was assigned to at the front. The work was easier than the hard labor others had to perform, and occasionally he got extra food from some of the officers he worked for.

During my father's absence, his partner and friend, Uncle Jóska, who was Catholic, owned and operated the store (with my mother's help). Jews were not allowed to own property, and in time, Jews were not allowed to accept employment either, so eventually my mother had to stop working there. Uncle Jóska and his wife, Auntie Lisa, who was a housewife, ended up having to run the store by themselves as best they could till the end of the war. They were great friends who never exploited the situation to their own personal gain, but continued to support our family financially, at great peril to their own safety.

I don't recall much about those years (between 1942 and 1945), other than a few images, and, obviously, my parents never liked to talk about their experiences during that period. Later, when I would question them, they would respond with specific answers to what I asked, but then they would quickly change the subject. Seeing their obvious discomfort, I stopped asking questions. Now I wish I had persevered.

I learned later that we had to move out of our comfortable home into an apartment house with a big yellow Star of David painted above the front door. It was reserved for Jews only and located in the Jewish district. I remember sitting with my brother on a two-wheeled cart on top of a few of our essential possessions, clutching my beloved Katie doll with her beautiful blue eyes, being wheeled around by my mother through the cobblestone streets till we reached our destination. We started out after lunch, with an emotional sendoff from Auntie Mariska, but it was after dark when we arrived in the small two-room apartment we shared with two other families. About eight of us children slept in one bedroom, mostly on the floor, while the mothers occupied the other one. The fathers were all away in labor battalions or fighting in the underground. I obviously didn't understand what was happening, but I felt uncomfortable in the cramped quarters with all those strangers around, and I sensed my mother's insecurity and profound unhappiness.

We hardly ever went outside, and we had only basic cooked meals, like beans, green peas, potatoes, and bread with lard, nothing like Auntie Mariska's treats. She found employment with a Christian family and visited us occasionally, despite the danger this defiant act presented to her own safety, bringing special meals and cookies. As time passed, we learned that buildings like ours, which housed only Jews, were gradually being emptied of their occupants by the Nazi SS troops. People were carted off to concentration camps, never to be seen again. My mother was determined that we should escape that fate. She knew we had to leave if we were to survive, and after about six months, she did manage to find a way out.

At some point in the spring of 1944, with the help of Aunt Eva's husband, who was in the underground, my mother was able to obtain false identifications for the three of us, and we moved into a nice bright apartment overlooking the Danube River. On the forged documents, we were identified as being the relatives from the provincial town of Györ of the elderly Christian couple who had been renting the apartment for years and were still there. Aunt Eva, with her daughter, Andy, and Aunt Ika with her daughter, Zita, were also hiding out with different families in the same building. As I piece the stories together, I suspect the building might have been one of the "safe houses" that Raoul Wallenberg, the Swedish envoy, established with help from underground organizations to save Jewish families from extermination. Today there is a street in the neighborhood named after this courageous diplomat, who reportedly died in a Russian prison in Siberia.

One day, members of the SS Nazi troupe came to search the building. They were looking for Jews with false identification. Although at the time I did not understand what was happening, this episode is my most frightening memory of the war. People were lined up in the hallways, young and old, with papers in hand. The boys, my brother among them, were hidden somewhere in the cellars below in the basement. In those days, only Jewish boys were circumcised, making them easily identifiable. To have them exposed to the possibility of a physical inspection would have been too dangerous for everybody involved.

But I was there, at the end of the line, a little girl dressed in blue (my favorite color), standing against the wall, clutching my beautiful Katie doll with one hand and hanging on to my mother's hand with the other. This towering uniformed SS guard stood in front of us. Even today, I can still see his mean figure silhouetted against the window, his black uniform, his black cap pulled over his forehead. He was so powerful, so menacing, that I can still feel an overpowering fear envelop me. He held a black leather nightstick, which he tapped against his huge, shiny black leather boot, in his right hand. All I could do was stare at those big black boots while I played with the little white lace booties on my doll's feet. *One, two, three, four* … I was counting the taps of his nightstick till I could count no more. Then our evening prayer came to my mind, "My God, Good God…," and I started silently reciting it over and over in rhythm to the tap of his nightstick, until slowly my overwhelming anxiety seemed to subside. To this day, black leather boots make me feel very uncomfortable.

Although the officers found all the tenants' papers in order, for some reason they became suspicious of Aunt Ika's behavior and took her with them for questioning. This frightened the whole house. As it turned out, she was put into jail at some barracks. Following the initial interrogation, which she refused to talk about afterwards, the authorities seem to have lost interest in her. Within a month, an underground organization smuggled her out of prison and sent her to another safe house in a provincial city till the end of the war.

After the inspection, my mother was afraid to stay in that house. "They will come back," she kept saying with justifiable fear, "and next time we will not be so lucky." She began desperately searching for a safer place. Eventually, she managed to place my brother and me in an exclusive Christian Evangelical orphanage, while she moved in with friends of Uncle Jóska in another part of town. Using her false identity, she found part time employment as a bookkeeper in an exclusive restaurant, the Gundel.

Around the same time, she decided to have the whole family convert to the Christian Evangelical faith. There must have been a combination of reasons that led her to that decision, some practical, some spiritual, as well as gratitude for the church's willingness to offer her children a sanctuary in the face of deadly danger.

In spite of all the hardships my mother had to endure, she still looked many years younger than her true age. She was still beautiful, with hazel eyes, light brown hair, and a petite, slim figure. Soon, against her best intentions, she attracted a German army officer as an ardent suitor. Tall, blond, with intelligent, blue eyes peering from behind wire-rimmed spectacles, he cut an imposing figure in his uniform. He didn't like Hitler and his policies, and he didn't agree with the war, but realizing he was trapped, he tried to do his duty and make the best of his circumstances. He was an intellectual who was impressed as much by my mother's intelligence as by her beauty. He would bring her flowers and food, and despite her repeated refusals and rejections of his advances, he asked her to marry him.

My mother had been renting a room in a second floor apartment when the building she and the German officer both lived in collapsed on top of her during an allied bombing raid. Later, my mother would make light of the terror she must have felt just before the impact of the bomb that hit her building. When you are under frequent bombardment, eventually you can tell how far the bombs are from where you are by the sound they make as they fall toward the earth. She joked that she could tell that it had her address inscribed on it as the bull's eye.

On being notified of the hit, the German officer immediately dispatched his unit to the site. Scores of Germans were digging with their bare hands to remove debris, and after hours of searching, they were able to locate and rescue my mother from under the rubble of twisted steel, concrete, and bricks. She had been pinned under a steel beam in an air pocket under the ruins, hoping and praying that she could be found and saved. She suffered only a broken arm and some cuts and bruises. Shortly after that incident, the officer and his unit was ordered to the front, where he died in an ambush, never to find out that the love of his life was of Jewish descent. Although my mother said a prayer for him, she did not mourn for him, for according to her pragmatic approach to life at the time, all he represented was one less German to be afraid of. After her rescue, my mother seemed to enjoy discussing the irony of the situation: that she owed her survival to a bunch of German soldiers.

It was very dangerous for my mother to visit us at the orphanage without putting her new identity in jeopardy. She managed to do so only a few times, bringing food and chocolates for us and the other children.

During the winter of 1944-45, as the Germans were pushed farther and farther back towards the west, our lives became very miserable. The siege of Budapest began on Christmas Eve and lasted fifty-one days before the Russians managed to capture the city. In January, there were constant air raids at night, and we all slept on the floor of the cold basement in our winter coats, hats, and gloves while the bombs kept falling. There was no gas, no electricity, and the water pipes froze shut. We had to melt snow for drinking water. Most of the time, we were hungry, cold, and sick, without any hope for relief. Not only was there the ever-present danger of bombs falling from the sky, but in addition there were unexploded ordinances scattered on the ground. The effects of these terrible conditions on a seven-year-old girl last a lifetime. To this day, in addition to the actual physical discomfort, feeling hunger or cold affects me psychologically: I get terribly agitated and upset.

My brother had shrapnel wounds just below his right knee, which got infected and needed cleaning every day. My heart was aching for him. I stayed with him, holding him while the nurse cleaned and dressed his leg, trying to give him strength for the ordeal.

The orphanage was located on an elegant, wide, tree-lined road called Fasor, meaning "a row of trees." It led from the center of Pest to the outskirts. Early one morning, one of the boys spotted a dead horse lying in the snow. A hand grenade had killed it during the night. All the children were sent out with knives to carve themselves as much meat as they could before other people found and took it. We went in happy anticipation of a good meat dinner for that night, cheerfully reciting the well-known Hungarian proverb, "He, who rises early is the one who finds gold." I remember getting a piece of his hind leg. I didn't want to go near his head, though, for I was afraid to have to look at his eyes, even though one of the boys told me that that's how you knew for sure that he was dead.

Most of the time the standard food staple was a bowl of cooked beans, potatoes, or peas, as the orphanage seemed to have a supply of those, as well as flour for baking rye bread. However, we had a veritable feast that night with a delicious "horse-*paprikás*," a Hungarian stew, usually prepared with chicken, pork, veal, or beef. Adding to our joy was the fact that we were allowed to eat as much as we wanted, in contrast to the rationed meals we were accustomed to.

Once the Germans were pushed back from our area to the river and the Russians took over, life became a little better. We could go outside to collect wood for fires in the stoves that heated the rooms, and we could also play on the grounds in the snow without having to worry about stray bullets and bombs, although the danger of unexploded ordinances was ever present.

Early one morning ("He who rises early..."), somebody found a huge jar of strawberry jam by the sidewalk. It must have fallen off an army supply truck. What a treat! What joy, a slice of bread with strawberry jam spread on it! Since that day, a slice of bread generously spread with strawberry jam remains a cherished treat for me. Eventually, relief agencies gave the orphanage jars of peanut butter, which was spread generously on bread slices for its nutritional value, and peanut butter became our standard food staple for a long, long time. I have not eaten any peanut butter since my orphanage days.

Hungary was "liberated" from the Germans by the Soviet Army in the spring of 1945 and optimistically embarked on the road to recovery and reconstruction. My father came back from the front, my parents began to rebuild their lives, and we were allowed to return to our old apartment as the lawful occupants. Auntie Mariska, our old housekeeper, rejoined the family as well, reclaiming her rightful place as the supreme ruler of the kitchen.

In anticipation of the Russian army's reported looting, Uncle Jóska and his friends hid most of the merchandise in the cellar below the shop, which seemed like a smart move, as on several occasions, bands of soldiers looted the store for whatever they could find. However, this precaution later backfired when a water main broke and flooded the cellar, damaging valuable materials. My father and Uncle Jóska counted their losses and salvaged what they could.

My father took trips by freight train to the rural areas to peddle his wares in exchange for staples such as flour, beans, peas, chicken, eggs, cheese, butter—any food items he could get. Since inflation raged and paper money was useless, he had to trade the store's merchandise for food. These were very dangerous trips, for in addition to all the robbers roaming the countryside; the Russians were looking for healthy men to transport to Siberia as laborers. To survive these trips, he had to disguise himself as a poor old man dressed in rags, with an unkempt beard. For quite a while, my mother seldom ventured out. It was dangerous for women, even cleverly disguised ones, for the Russian soldiers were wandering the streets, looting and raping. It rapidly became clear to the people of Budapest that the Russian army had no concerns beyond its immediate physical needs.

Nevertheless, conditions began to normalize after the war. My father started rebuilding the store and my mother found employment again as a bookkeeper, which provided a small, but steady income. Knowing that millions had died, they felt blessed for having been given the opportunity to pick up the debris caused by the war and reconstruct their lives.

Today, I can't even imagine how my parents managed to come through this horrible period, how they found the fortitude and resourcefulness to overcome all the danger, the hardship, losses, and disappointments. Somehow, through all that adversity, they succeeded. We survived, and, slowly, they rebuilt our lives to the level it had been before the war. Viewing their accomplishments with gratitude and awe, I can only guess what made them so strong. Possibly they drew strength from their unshakable belief that good must ultimately triumph over evil. Or perhaps they had an unwavering faith in a future where—in a better world—their descendants would benefit from the fruits of their labor.

Chapter Four

ELEMENTARY SCHOOL YEARS

After the Second World War, between 1945 and 1949, with the elected government's aim of establishing a "people's democracy," Hungary's political system underwent several radical changes. The dozen or so political parties formed after the war were reduced to four by 1948, at which time the Social Democrats and the Communists merged to form the all-powerful Hungarian Working People's Party. However, the Moscow-bred Communist, Mátyás Rákosi, and his associates managed to grab power by executing and imprisoning their rivals within the government. They established absolute power under a Stalinist state. These so-called Moscovites centralized economic policies and enforced the collectivization of agriculture, the nationalization of privately held factories, and the rapid development of heavy industry. As these drastic measures were slowly taking hold, Rákosi and his henchmen also began to intimidate small-scale businesses and to appropriate their often-small assets. In addition to show trials, which helped eliminate their rivals, they developed secret personal dossiers, and educational discrimination against children on the basis of social class became the prevailing practice.

Despite my parents' interest in politics, I was not aware of the changes that were to affect my future. For me, school was great fun from day one, and I consistently did well because I took my studies seriously. All my life, I have loved going to school. My parents, especially my father, cared a great deal about education. From our earliest years, they explained to us in great detail about the importance of learning and acquiring knowledge, contrasting it with ignorance, which was a lack of knowledge, a condition that can and should be overcome. They described the undesirable consequences of ignorance, illustrating them with examples from family, friends, and history. "Knowledge is power," my father would tell us. "The only thing they can't take away from you is what is inside your head," he would repeat over and over through the years. Every day, our father and mother would question us about school, look at our homework, and help us study. Just as he did while I was wrapping merchandise in the store when I was younger, my father would say to us, "If it is worth doing, it is worth doing well." He would admonish us each time he thought our work wasn't good enough until we persevered and earned his praise for a job well done. I never stopped feeling that school was important, that the work I was doing was important; and, that it was important to do it well.

In the fall of 1945, our parents decided to send us to a combined first and second grade class at the parochial school run by the evangelical church, even though there was a public elementary school located four blocks from our house. My brother went to the school for boys next to the orphanage on Fasor Street, while I went to the one for girls on Deák Court. The schools were in different parts of the city, and both of us needed to take a streetcar to get there. We were each put in the charge of an older student, who, for a slight fee, was responsible for our safety during our commute to school.

Sunday mornings, decked out in our school uniforms and accompanied most of the time by our mother, my brother and I both attended services at the cathedral on Deák Court. This was the only time the girls' classes from Deák Court met those of the boys from Fasor.

During one church service, for some reason my friends and I just could not stop giggling. We were sitting in the front, by class, in alphabetical order, and distracted by the minister's appearance and mannerisms, which we found comical, we were not able to follow his words. But we had gotten his attention, right in the middle of his sermon. He was shouting, flailing his arms, stabbing his finger in the air, trying to make a point that made no sense to us. One of us must have made a funny remark, and the giggles started and couldn't be stopped. Accompanied by our embarrassed homeroom teacher, Auntie Piroska, we had to go to the sacristy after the service for a thorough reprimand. I adored Auntie Piroska, who was young and pretty. I felt horrible about putting her in a position where she was being reproved for my misbehavior. Afterward, she had a talk with us, one at a time. She seemed to understand, and after some discussion, and our promises of better self-control, to my great relief, she forgave us. One day she even asked me to stay after school and help her grade some math papers. What an honor! For the three years I spent under her wing, she continued to be the strict, but loving and fair teacher whom I wanted to please and emulate.

In those days, the European school environment was very different from what students experience in today's classrooms. There were strict rules regarding conduct and academic performance, and parents were held accountable for both their children's behavior and home assignments. During class, when we had no reading or writing to do, we had to sit quietly with our hands crossed behind our backs at waist height. In response to questions, we had to silently raise our right hand in a fist with the index and middle fingers extended and wait patiently in that position until called on by the teacher.

Since in our family, education was of utmost importance, my brother and I were expected to behave and perform well in school. We were given generous rewards for good grades and conduct and kept under constant threat of punishment for the slightest transgression. My parents often helped us with our schoolwork. I remember my mother and father drilling us on our math facts for hours on end. I remember them watching over us as we practiced our penmanship, writing and rewriting assignments until every curve, every letter looked like the printed page we were to copy. My mother spent a lot of time helping us with reading until we became proficient readers; then she concentrated on grammar and composition.

As part of the prescribed curriculum, both my brother and I took religion classes at our schools and had our confirmation and first communion at the Cathedral. On Sunday mornings during the summers, Auntie Mariska would take me to various Catholic churches in the city. I especially loved to attend the high services on Castle Hill in Buda at historical St Matthias Church, which was named after one of Hungary's great monarchs. I didn't understand the Latin mass, but I let myself float with the magnificent organ music by composers such as Bach, Mozart, and Liszt. I let my mind wander and my imagination take flight. Sometimes I would try to picture all the ancient, noble ladies in their finery, sitting in the ornate, hand carved row of chairs by the altar. Other times, I would amuse myself by watching the people around me, inventing lives for them based on their appearance.

Visiting a house of worship, any one of God's homes, regardless of the denomination, was an important part of my life. I felt a deep sense of obligation to God for having spared us, together with wonder as to His purpose.

My experiences during the war made me appreciate the gift of life and the importance of believing in the existence of a supreme being. In my mind, God was everywhere. He was the one I turned to with my gratitude, my wishes, and my problems every night before I fell asleep. He was also the one to whom I turned at other times, in other places, between church visits as the need would strike me. Since God had saved me during the war, I was convinced He would stand by me as long as I worked at being the best me I could possibly be. I always believed that God was on my side and that my God wanted me to succeed in life and be happy.

During the summer, when we were eleven years old, my father, who was an avid sportsman, had enrolled my brother and me in private swimming lessons at the Palatinus Pool, which was on the far end of Margaret Island. Usually, we had to take a bus across the bridge to the pool, but sometimes we walked to the ferry and crossed the Danube by boat.

The swim master, as the teacher was called then, taught us the breaststroke first. We were suspended from the side of the pool in a harness lowered into the water, where we had to perform the movements and breathe precisely as we had practiced on dry land beforehand. My mother never learned how to swim—she didn't even like the water—but she faithfully took us to the pool every day and cheered us on as we progressed. After our lessons, we would sit on the large well-kept grassy area and eat the sandwiches Auntie Mariska had lovingly prepared for us that morning. When we did really well, which, as I recall, was almost every day, my mother would buy us ice cream. By the end of the summer, we both became good swimmers at breaststroke and backstroke. Ever since then, both swimming and music have played very important parts in my life. I have been swimming for exercise all my life, reaping the physical benefits as well as the psychological and intellectual ones. Gliding in the water can be very relaxing, and I seem to get my best ideas while watching the bottom of the pool pass by.

After fifth grade, in 1948, Johnny and I found ourselves back in the neighborhood public elementary school, together with many other children who also had to transfer back from Catholic, Jewish, and private schools. The government was nationalizing all nonpublic schools and children were required to attend their assigned district schools. Even though I was heartbroken over having to part with Auntie Piroska and most of my classmates from Deák Court, I was looking forward to being in school with some of my old friends from the area where we lived.

The public school was located on a street corner, in a huge, stone, five-story building that was four city blocks from my house. The boys' entrance was on *Sziget* (Island) Street, whereas the girls had to go round the corner to the right for their entrance. On some days, it became quite an ordeal for girls to pass the boys' side because of the loud, sarcastic, unkind comments the boys made. Many girls chose to take a longer, roundabout way home to avoid potential harassment from the boys. I did not have that problem, however, because my gallant brother and his friends, who were also my friends, ensured an undisturbed passage for my friends and me at all times.

I continued to do very well in my studies at the new school and received top marks most of the time on my tests and home assignments. I did particularly well in mathematics. My math teacher, Auntie Margit, was especially strict with us girls. She made sure we kept up with the boys' classes. She would keep students after school for tutorials, with some of the better ones (myself included) helping out for extra credit. I gained great self-confidence from these sessions, for I discovered that not only was I good in mathematics, but that I could explain it well to others and that I enjoyed the process. Soon I developed a reputation as a good math tutor, and students started to seek me out for help with their homework outside of these tutorials. Many times, I found myself gaining deeper insights as a result of trying to teach concepts and processes to my peers. Even that early, I found teaching a very enjoyable and rewarding experience.

One day in a grade six geography class, as we were studying the republics of the "Great Soviet Socialist Union," I felt a headache coming on. It was stronger than the usual ones I had been experiencing lately. I was getting nauseated, and sparks began to fly around in front of my eyes. I could feel the blood drain out of my head and I passed out. I was taken to the nurse's office. A doctor was called, and he recommended a thorough physical and neurological examination, especially on noticing a slight tremor in my hands. I had been aware of the gradual unsteadiness of my hands for some time, but I never attached much significance to it, especially since I noticed that my father's hands trembled occasionally and my brother's hands were not steady either. Eventually, the headaches were judged to be migraines caused by stress, and the tremors a hereditary affliction of unknown origin. I was told to relax and learn to live with both conditions for the rest of my life.

Around that time, my parents bought a big, black, upright piano, and I started piano lessons once a week. My teacher lived two blocks from my home, on the ground floor in a gorgeous apartment, where her grand piano sat in the corner of a large living room in front of the huge bay window. In the summers, you could hear the music streaming through the open window as you passed by the building. She had several extremely talented students, and I realized that I had only modest abilities. Despite that, I enjoyed playing and continued to practice diligently, even with the knowledge that I didn't have what it takes to have a musical career.

One of these eminent students, Peter Frankel, went on to international acclaim in piano performance and teaching. Another, György Pauk, did the same with his violin. Johnny started with lessons, too, but he stopped in no time, while I continued for eight years, till after my graduation from high school. I am glad I did, for all my life, music has been my constant companion, providing solace, comfort, and joy.

Occasionally I would meet Viktor, the son of one of my mother's friend I used to like as a little girl. Depending on the season, we would go for a walk and talk or go skating or to a movie. There was a small movie theater near our house, where he took me one day to see the favorite movie of my childhood, the American film *Sun Valley Serenade*, starring Sonja Henie. He knew I would like it because of all the wonderful skating and the music of Glenn Miller. The movie was romantic, and as he walked me home, he confided in me that he was going to be a famous jazz pianist and composer and that he was hoping that I would marry him when we grew up. Here I was, barely eleven years old, and I already had a marriage proposal! We kissed each other good-bye on the cheeks as we parted, a gesture that became a reaffirmation of our childhood affection each time our paths would cross for the rest of our lives.

My very best friend throughout primary school was Susie Kosály, a pretty, bubbly girl with a permanent mischievous twinkle in her eyes. Regardless of what we were doing, I always had fun when we were together. She knew a lot about boys from her older sister, who was popular with them in a different way from me. Perhaps because of my twin brother, I was just the boys' friend. It was she to whom I ran in great panic one day when I discovered blood on my panties, and it was she who explained all about the birds and the bees, including the details my mother was too embarrassed to talk about.

Susie was very artistic and planned to become a fashion designer—not a very realistic aspiration in a communist society. She was determined to persevere in developing her talents in that direction. She started making her own dresses at a very young age, with help from her aunt who was an accomplished seamstress. Her outfits were always unusual and pretty, at least in my eyes.

Although for some periods before and after the war, life was good for Susie's family, her life turned out to be even more difficult than mine. She and her older sister, Judy, lived with their parents in a lovely apartment with a view of the Danube River from their balcony. However, suddenly there was a knock on the door in the middle of the night. They were given twenty-four hours by the secret police to gather their belongings and be gone from their home. Before the communists came into power, her father had been a commodity trader. He was labeled a "capitalist," which was an undesirable element of the new socialist society. Now, because her parents were "displaced" to a small village in the country, Susie lived with an aunt on the ring road. "Mark my words," she would tell me confidently, "the communists will not last long. The Americans will eventually put an end to their rule." Even though I couldn't share her optimism, I kept hoping she was right for both of our sakes. Every day, we used to walk home together from school. We also went to an occasional movie together, we went skating in the winter, and we shared many confidences over the years.

The summer after sixth grade, my father enrolled us with a swim team that practiced at the sports pool complex on the near end of Margaret Island. After a while, since the pool was within walking distance from our house (about two miles), we were allowed to go to practices by ourselves. The children's coach was a friend of my father's, and he kept an eye on us. We learned to swim freestyle, to dive, and to do flip turns. Neither of us was winning competitions, but we liked the practices and the team spirit, so we kept going. After morning practice, we would hang around on the grassy knoll, eating Auntie Mariska's sandwiches and some fruit or buying an occasional ice cream, then at one o'clock we would head home. In the afternoons I would practice my piano or read or play with friends.

For a couple of summers, we also got to spend two or three weeks with a peasant family in a small village called Csorvás in the southeastern part of the country. This was great fun! We ran around barefoot, got to see how food is grown, and performed chores. I collected eggs, milked cows, churned butter, and made cheese. I also took the geese and ducks to pasture and picked vegetables and fruits to sell at the market on Saturdays. I especially loved picking tomatoes and eating them sun kissed, warm, and fresh off the vine. I wish every child could have the advantage of spending some time on a farm. It is a great experience!

Through the years, I continued to enjoy Uncle Jóska's frequent visits, his companionship, and our discussions. He liked music, and as I was growing up, he started taking me to the theater, concerts, and the opera. I respected his intelligence and valued his friendship and his constant encouragement. I also appreciated his generosity to our family, especially his courageous help during the war. Suddenly, however, in early 1949, he began to act very strangely. He was only about fifty years old, yet this brilliant man began to forget things and at times act confused and unpredictable. One evening he showed up at the opera with only half his face shaved. As his condition deteriorated rapidly, he went to the hospital for tests. He never left the hospital, for he was diagnosed with a serious brain tumor.

When I went to visit him with my mother in the hospital before his surgery, hoping to cheer up the beloved friend who had cheered me up so many times during my childhood, I came away heartbroken. By then, despite my best efforts, Uncle Jóska was unable to recognize me. He just lay there in a world of his own, where I was now a stranger. I proudly showed him my very first, brand new nylon stockings, with the black seam running along the back of my leg. However, he could not grasp the significance of a twelve-year old girl's first stockings, and he started gently stroking my legs as he would a statue's. When he died a few days later, after an unsuccessful operation, his death left a big void in my heart. I realized that to him I was the daughter he never had, and I mourned him as I would mourn a lost father.

My father bought out Uncle Jóska's share in the store from Auntie Lisa, his widow, who had no interest in the business, and moved the store from fashionable Váci Street—which, under the increasingly proletariat ideology, was losing its luster and importance—to a busy location near the eastern railway station. In addition to keeping his shrinking professional clientele, my father was hoping to attract business from the peasant population that visited the capital by train. His hope was fulfilled, as for a short while business picked up and he was happy, although deep down he knew that barring some miracle, the business wouldn't last.

Sure enough, as the Communist government continued to squeeze small entrepreneurs by continuous harassment and the selective raising of taxes, in 1950 my father lost his business, and this time he lost it for good. The dream he had had as a young man, the small enterprise he built through a lifetime of hard work, one that a world war, German SS brigades, Russian soldiers, bombs, and flooding couldn't destroy—this dream the communists obliterated. Eventually, my father had to liquidate his business, and as a "class outsider" (as small businessmen were labeled by the communists) he was forced to seek employment as a common laborer for a minimum wage.

In grade seven, I befriended Clara, a new girl in class, and took her under my wings, helping her with schoolwork every day. Her father, a hard-line communist, who had emigrated to Canada after the 1919 Soviet-style revolution in Hungary had been crushed, had just transplanted the family back from Canada in anticipation of the communists' rise to power again in Hungary. The family received a beautiful apartment from the state, one that became (or was made) available as a result of another, less desirable family being "displaced" to the countryside. Clara's family rapidly became the darlings of the Communist Party and the Pioneer Youth Organization. Their home and everything in it looked prosperous to me. Clara and her brother had gorgeous clothes, pencils, pens, books, and toys they had brought with them from Canada. I could not imagine why these people would leave a free, rich country like Canada to come and live with the hardships and injustices we had to endure here in Hungary. However, I kept my mouth shut and diligently worked with her. Clara and her younger brother spoke hardly any Hungarian, only English. To my great delight, she wasn't the only one who did the learning. I began to pick up words, then phrases in English, and eventually I learned to sing *Somewhere over the rainbow, way up high, there's a land that I heard of once in a lullaby...* I learned to play the melody on my piano as well, softly singing the words over and over behind closed doors. Soon I began to dream of that land, where *skies are blue*, where *bluebirds fly,* where the *dreams that you dare to dream really do come true...*

As I progressed through grades six, seven, and eight, the final year of primary school, I became increasingly apprehensive about my future. Not surprisingly, the frequency and severity of my migraine headaches increased as well. Although I was an excellent student, being the daughter of a "class outsider" had made my chances of being accepted into a good high school for further study pretty slim. I joined the Young Pioneers (a communist Scout organization), but of course, the "social outcast" label followed me there, too. Most of the time we did not have to wear our Soviet style uniforms—the blue skirt with the white blouse—only the red triangular Pioneer handkerchief tied around our neck. I didn't feel comfortable being a Pioneer, especially after an incident during one of our frequent after-school meetings. At these sessions we were required to study and analyze Marxist-Leninist communist ideology and relate it to our past, present, and future lives. My father's short definition of these topics was "political rubbish."

At one of these meetings, we were discussing an obscure Soviet writer's novel we had been required to read. It was about the daring deeds of Pavlik Morozov, a Russian Pioneer, who served his community by exposing his grandfather, a Kulak who had been hiding wheat from the people and hoping to sell it later for profit. Of course Pavlik was presented to us as a hero, a role model to follow. The group leader, a Communist Party functionary, asked for volunteers to practice self-criticism in relation to the story and to speak about the "correct" ideology we were to follow in our lives. To my surprise, a classmate, who had been a shy, withdrawn loner, raised her hand and proceeded to confess in a barely audible voice that her parents secretly listened to the BBC and Voice of America short-wave radio broadcasts in the evening, and she could not convince them to stop. As she finished this confession, there was a collective intake of breath in the room, followed by complete silence, with most of us looking at the floor, afraid to show our true feelings. As far as I knew, almost everybody listened secretly to the BBC or the Voice of America to get a balanced view of world events. However, officially, any news other than that from the state-run radio was determined to be "subversive imperialist propaganda."

While the group leader proceeded to praise her for her courage in speaking up, the rest of us could only stare at her in disbelief. I could feel my hands trembling as I clasped them together, while my best friend Susie sat next to me, motionless as a statue. We all knew that listening to western radio stations was dangerous. It was considered to be "a crime against the state," and some kind of appropriate punishment was sure to follow. Our apprehension was not misplaced. Within a couple of days, the girl's parents were picked up by the secret police. After being interrogated, they were "displaced" to a small country village, and as "enemies of the state," they lost their apartment, their jobs, and all their rights in Budapest. The young girl herself never recovered from the incident. Because her parents became destitute, she had to go live with her grandparents. However, as we learned later, she soon realized the grave consequences of her action and was terribly guilt-stricken. Within a year, she committed suicide by jumping out of the sixth floor apartment window where she lived, thus ending a promising, but tragically short life.

Despite that tragedy and the social conflicts swirling around me, I enjoyed going to school. Thanks to the influence of my wonderful mathematics teacher, Auntie Margit, during the last three years of primary school, by seventh grade I had gradually resolved what I wanted to choose as my future profession. I decided to become a mathematics teacher, even though the obstacles looming on the horizon to that goal seemed insurmountable.

For one thing, even though my father was working now as a common laborer in a toy factory for meager hourly wages, I was still considered to be the descendant of a "social outcast." As such, I was not entitled to higher education, until all descendants of the working proletariat had their educational choices honored. In addition, my parents did not want me to become a teacher, for they felt that teachers were the slaves of society and had to work extremely hard for a small salary.

Since I was pretty good in science as well as in mathematics, and I was fascinated by physics, electricity, and radios, after some family discussion, it was decided that I should apply to the Kando Kálmán Villamosipari Technikum. This was a unique, prestigious, technical secondary school named after a famed Hungarian physicist. In addition to preparing its graduates for university admission, this school also awarded an electrical engineering technician diploma, qualifying students for specific engineering positions in industry. This compromise seemed acceptable to me and my parents, who felt reassured that I would have a marketable profession upon graduation from high school. I was satisfied because the decision did not shut the door for a university education later. The door was still open for me to become a mathematics teacher.

However, just as we feared, all the discussions, all the planning, all my good grades, and all my work with the Pioneer organization turned out to be for naught. When the list of high school admissions was posted, despite my straight A's, my name was relegated to a neighborhood general secondary school, which would lead me nowhere. The curriculum it offered was not strong enough to qualify students for studies at any university, but provided only a general education that prepared students only for office work. Even worse, my brother, whose grades were less than stellar, was listed for a trade school as a plumber's apprentice.

I was crushed, frustrated, and angry. Although I tried to put on a cheerful face during the day for my parents' sake, I cried myself to sleep every night. Despite all our efforts, the future seemed bleak for us both—for the "smart brother" and his "industrious sister"—indeed, for the whole family. "Is this what God saved us for during the war?" I asked desperately. But there was no answer and there seemed to be no way out. My father had many friends, some in good positions, but they either couldn't or wouldn't help. Sticking one's neck out for the daughter of a "social outcast" was not a politically smart move. There was an official appeals process, and I went through it in full knowledge of the predictable outcome. Summer came, and for the first time in my life, I was not looking forward to the vacation and the new school year starting in September.

Before graduation in March of 1951, we had celebrated our fourteenth birthdays, which meant that we were allowed to work. That summer, my mother, who was employed as a bookkeeper by the hospitality industry, was able to secure me a steady part-time position selling ice cream from a booth in front of the national circus. The building that housed the circus was situated between the Budapest Zoo and the amusement park, and was located in a large park called Városliget. On days when the weather was nice, people milled around with their children, trying to enjoy the moment and forget their cares and make their outing a happy occasion. I tried to take part in the festivities too, but my problems kept intruding. I didn't mind selling ice cream. I met a lot of interesting people and the extra money was a relief for the family budget, but doing it as a career didn't appeal to me at all.

Furthermore, working in an office for the rest of my life, pushing papers around seemed even a worse fate. I was not going to resign myself to what I considered to be a life of mediocrity. I was convinced I could make a meaningful contribution to humanity, and I wanted a chance to try. The more I thought about it, the more preoccupied I became with finding a solution that would provide me with the education I needed and felt I was entitled to. I had been a good student all my life. I became obsessed with the need to try and make something happen. As I realized that I had to find a way to get into a good school by September, my frustration grew. I didn't know how I could accomplish my goal. At night, when all was quiet, I would often sit by my open window and look up at the patch of sky with its countless stars visible above the courtyard searching for a solution. I can still hear myself singing, *"When you wish upon a star..."*

Chapter Five

SECONDARY SCHOOL YEARS

By the time of my graduation from primary school in the spring of 1951, Mátyás Rákosi and his Moscow-bred associates were enjoying absolute power in a Stalinist police state of Hungary. Although he was a Soviet citizen, Rákosi was portrayed in the official Hungarian literature of the time as the "people's wise leader" and the "father of our country." Born in Hungary, but having spent most of his life in the Soviet Union, he was a fervent admirer and true disciple of the Russian dictator, Josef Stalin. He was well known for being ruthless in supporting Moscow's stranglehold on Hungary and for ferociously promoting communist ideology. Between 1948 and 1953, the Hungarian economy was reorganized according to the Soviet model and all social and economic planning was centralized, with about ninety-nine percent of all workers becoming employees of the state. In 1949, the regime held a single-candidate election, and on August 20 of that year the government ratified a Soviet-style constitution. The country was rapidly sinking into a depression, and living conditions for most of its citizens were deteriorating. Improvements that had been made after the war, from 1945 on, were gradually erased after the communists took over in 1948 in what was labeled by them as the great "turning point."

As we approached the summer of 1951, there seemed to be no hope, no way out for our family. My parents' combined income was barely enough to feed and house us, while the long-cherished educational goals for us children seemed out of reach forever. Due to the nature of the schools we were assigned to by the state, instead of becoming a scientist, I was destined to become an office worker or sales clerk, and instead of becoming an engineer, my brother was slated to become a workman's apprentice in the construction industry. The whole family was depressed, but Auntie Mariska was outright furious. "I'll go see that SOB Mátyás Rákosi personally to tell him what I think of him," she fumed, "especially for preventing my twins from getting the quality education they deserve. The idiot. It's bad enough that he's bankrupting this nation by sending its resources off to the Soviet Union, but now, in addition, he's depriving the country of a brilliant future scientist and engineer. Does he know what's going on? Somebody should inform him, this so-called father of his country, because a father shouldn't, couldn't, wouldn't, do this to his children."

The phrase, "somebody should inform him" stuck in my mind and gave birth to an idea. What if I wrote Rákosi a letter and appealed to him personally for help? I might make things happen, I reasoned to myself, rather than just sit back and let things happen to me by default.

In a family council, we considered the consequences of my writing such a letter and decided that we didn't have much to lose, but much to gain and that the possible benefits far outweighed the potential harm. Unfortunately, I do not have a copy of the original letter I wrote; the following is only an approximate reconstruction.

Dear Comrade Rákosi!

As one would ask for help from his father in a time of need, I, Julianna Adler, a fourteen-year- old Pioneer, am turning to you, the father of our country for support in my plight.

I aspire to be a scientist when I grow up, to help our country become a prosperous Communist state, a worthwhile partner of the great Soviet Union. So far I have worked hard in developing my talents. This spring I graduated from primary school as a straight A student. Despite that achievement, I am finding myself excluded from the school of my choice, the Kando Kálmán Villamosipari Technikum. The problem seems to be my ancestry, which is something I have no control over. I can't change my past, but given the chance I know I can build a great future.

Please look into my case and use your influence to help me gain admission to the Kando Kálmán Villamosipari Technikum and I promise to work my hardest to become an exceptional scientist in the interest of the people of Hungary and the glory of our Communist state.

Thanking you in advance for your trouble,
Julianna Adler
Budapest, XIII
Pannonia utca 22, III emelet 6

When I mailed my letter the last week of July, the feeling of utter helplessness had lifted slightly. I had some hope now. We started counting the days, waiting breathlessly either for a favorable reply or a knock on the front door in the middle of the night from the dreaded AVO secret police. Auntie Mariska made an offering to her favorite saint, St Anthony, for his intercession on my behalf. Remembering the adage, "God helps those, who help themselves," I prayed day and night. Unwise as it was, I couldn't pass a church without sneaking in to light a candle for my special intention, especially if there were strains of organ music filtering out.

When finally the response came at the end of August in an official envelope from the Communist Party Secretariat, I held it in my hands for a long time, afraid to open it. Finally mustering the courage to look, I found with relief that the news was good. There were two letters written by some obscure bureaucrat in the name of Mátyás Rákosi. One was addressed to the principal of the Kando Kálmán Villamosipari Technikum, instructing him to accept Julianna Adler in the incoming freshman class. The other was addressed to me and wished me good luck in my studies at my new school and in my career as a scientist. I would love to know if my letter ever got to Rákosi or if somebody in the Secretariat read it and had pity on this desperate, but brave young girl. Probably the latter is true, although as I remember, Rákosi's signature was affixed to the letter addressed to me. (On second thought, it might have been just a stamp.)

The letter came just in time, two days before school was to start. Next day I showed up early in the morning in the principal's office at the KKV Technikum, expecting no problems. Even though, on seeing my letter from the Communist Party Secretariat, the principal treated me with great deference, he informed me that at the moment the school simply had no room for an extra student in the freshman class. The school was located in an old building, with old furniture and old equipment. Taking me on a tour of the school, he said earnestly, "I would love to have you as a student here, but there is no way to put an extra desk in the classroom or an extra station in the laboratories and workshops." As we returned to his office, however, the principal was able to offer an alternate solution. "A year ago, a brand new school, the Budapesti Villamosenergiaipari Technikum opened to serve as an extension to our Technikum's program. I could call the principal there, who is a friend of mine, and see if he could find room for you at that school. You could start your studies there, and since the curriculum is the same in freshman year in both schools, you would have no problem transferring back to KKV Technikum once an opening becomes available."

"Send the darling right over," was the response of Mr. Takács, the principal of BVT Technikum. "I can use all the straight A students I can get!" he cheerfully exclaimed. I was sitting at the opposite side of the desk, yet his booming voice carried right through the telephone. I happily accepted, gathered up my transcripts, and headed for the other school, for what I hoped was to become my gateway to a promising future in a science-related career.

The new school, located in the northern suburbs of Budapest, truly impressed me. It was modern and bright and seemed much better equipped than the KKV Technikum. However, it didn't have the reputation KKV Technikum did, not yet, I thought. Instantly I took a liking to the principal, Dénes Takács, a kindly middle-aged gentleman with thin-rimmed spectacles, who (as I found out later) was all over the place, in and out of classrooms, talking to teachers and students throughout the day. He loved his job and his school, but above all, he loved his students and took a personal interest in their well-being.

With encouragement from my father, it took me two days to find the nerve to knock on the principal's door and ask for a private audience. I told him how grateful I was for having been accepted at his school and how happy I was to be there and how I loved it already. Then I explained to him how I got to be there and about my really smart twin brother, who wanted to be an electrical engineer, but was not given the opportunity because of our circumstances. "Bring your brother with you tomorrow before school, with all his papers for an interview," Mr. Takács told me, "and make sure he is ready to start classes if I accept him." That was the end of that. János was accepted as a student, too, on the spot.

That Sunday afternoon, the whole family celebrated with a special visit to the Gerbaud pastry shop, where I was allowed to choose from among many delicacies, such as the famous drum (*dobos*) cake, goose feet (*ludláb*), creampuff (*krémes*), chestnut purée with whipped cream, or ice cream in sugar cones. My father offered toasts with raspberry soda in honor of his daughter the *kis okos,* as my parents wished us good luck in our studies at our new school.

Later, at the close of the school year, I approached the principal once more, this time on behalf of my cousin, Eva, so she could be admitted to the next incoming freshman class, and again he said yes. By the time I was notified of an opening at KKV Technikum, I decided to stay at my present school and declined the offer to transfer.

My brother and I realized only much later that going to school together for the first time on that bright, sunny September morning in 1951 was the beginning of our rich and productive professional careers. At that time, we were oblivious to the fact that these were the first few steps taken by a future engineer and a future scientist who resolved early on in their lives to make a difference in the world.

The curriculum of the school was demanding and the teachers were firm but fair. I liked them all, especially the brilliant, mathematics teacher, a strict, but kind old man called Imre Pálos, whom we affectionately called *Spugyi bácsi* (this is a nonsense endearment). He was short and pudgy, with thick, graying hair, a gray mustache, and dark-rimmed spectacles, his piercing blue eyes peering out above them. The man was always impeccably dressed, with a white lab coat over his gray suit, white shirt, and a bowtie, commanding respect with his demeanor and appearance. He was fond of quoting the famous remark made by Menaechmus, a Greek mathematician, to Alexander the Great around 350 B.C.: "There is no royal road to Geometry." (Some sources credit Euclid with having said the quote first to his pupil Ptomely.) While encouraging his students to work through their difficulties, *Spugyi bácsi* would frequently alter the subject of the sentence by changing geometry into algebra, trigonometry, mathematics, or life in general. In his estimation, there was no royal road, no shortcut to anything worth having. His road to success was hard work. Under his expert direction, I learned the fundamentals of algebra, geometry and trigonometry with a functional approach, gaining a solid foundation for higher mathematics. He brought out the best in all his students by imparting to them a love for the subject, and I thrived under his guidance.

Our homeroom teacher, Auntie Balázs, who guided us through grades nine through twelve, taught us the Russian language. We hated the subject, even though we loved the teacher, and she knew it. She understood and secretly shared our sentiments, but learning Russian was compulsory and because we were required to pass both an oral and a written state exam on graduation to demonstrate mastery in it, she was strict with us. She was a highly educated, intelligent woman, with two diplomas, a most unusual accomplishment for a woman at that time. Having lost her husband during the war, she was the sole support for her three teenage children. Auntie Zita, as some of us privately called her, spoke six languages, yet in addition to those, she had had to learn Russian in a hurry if she wanted to continue teaching, for that was the only foreign language allowed to be taught in schools under the communist regime.

Classes ran from eight in the morning, to three or four o'clock in the afternoon, except on Saturdays, when classes were held from eight to one o'clock. We had Sundays off. The curriculum included four years of Hungarian language and literature, history, mathematics, physics, chemistry, art, physical education, and (of course) Russian. These were the regular courses in a college preparatory gymnasium. However, to complement these, over the years we had courses in descriptive geometry, technical drawing, strength of materials, electric motors, electric networks, radio technology, machine shop and the like. In addition to the long days at school, we had homework every day and about half an hour commute each way by tram. I was still a "good student," near the top of the class, but much as I tried, I could not be a straight-A student any more. Now I had to realize that I was far from perfect. Why I couldn't even be the best, but only one of the better ones. This was a notion that took some getting used to.

Although I struggled with many of the courses associated with mechanics and electricity, I excelled in history and the physics that I loved; Russian (ugh), which came easy; mathematics, which developed into the passion of my life; descriptive geometry, which I found fascinating because it awakened my sense of space; and technical drawing, which became the bread and butter of my early professional life.

Unfortunately, I had to face and accept the fact that I was one of the klutzy people in the machine shop. We had to work with lathes and saws, and I'll never forget the block of metal I was given. It was to be formed into a perfect cube using a metal file. When I filed one face, the adjoining face became too small. Then the opposite edges were not parallel, so I had to file some more, but then the edges were not smooth any more. So it went for hours and days that stretched into weeks. I think I filed at least three pieces of metal into oblivion, before I received an acceptable grade. If anything, the process taught me some patience. Of course, these days there is no need to teach humans to do these skills by hand; the task would be easily completed to perfection by preprogrammed machines.

Auntie Balázs lived two blocks away from us. To the discomfort of my brother, she wouldn't think twice about knocking on our door in the evening and complaining to my father about my brother's not infrequent transgressions. In those days few people had telephones, and notes home to parents didn't always make it home, so teachers had to rely on personal contacts. These visits always resulted in Johnny being "grounded" without the long-time desirable improvement in his behavior. Johnny is a free spirit, prone to act on impulse and talk back, especially when he thinks he is right (as he usually is), without worrying about the consequences. He had to learn diplomacy the hard way, how to survive to live and fight another day.

Stalin died in March of 1953, and on the day of his funeral, the whole nation was required to observe three minutes of silence at noon in his honor. We were in machine shop at the time, twenty-five teenagers in matching beige overalls standing quietly next to our workstations. The bright noon sun was streaming through the tiny basement window as I was gazing at the absolutely still street scene beyond. Slowly I became aware of the sounds of soft whistling to the strains of a patriotic Hungarian folk melody. The old master standing at the head of the class in his white lab coat, with his white hair and a smile on his face, filled the whole three minutes with his song. The remarkable thing about the incident was not his foolhardy courage, but the fact that nobody ever reported his defiant action. Like a flash of lightning, I suddenly realized that the communists were in trouble in Hungary, that despite all their efforts at indoctrination, they had lost the older generation and were not winning the hearts and minds of young people, either. As in many other times before during the history of this spirited, noble nation, Hungary would survive this Russian occupation. Standing there in the midst of the communist oppression, I knew with certainty that one day, we would be free again, and I began to look forward to that day.

Following the episode in the machine shop, I resumed my studies with renewed vigor. I also made a decision that was to have far-reaching consequences for the rest of my life, although at the time I did not recognize its true significance. For some inexplicable reason, which I never was able to explain, I decided that I wanted to learn English—in secret, of course. There was good reason for secrecy. Ordinary citizens were looked upon with suspicion for learning, or knowing western languages and I certainly could not afford to have another bad mark against me. Luckily, a language teacher, Mrs. Pálfalvi (Auntie Mici, as we called her), lived in the apartment above ours. Before the war, she had taught English, German, and French, but now she was retired, living with her bachelor son who was a respected scientist. She didn't charge much, she liked me, she knew we didn't have much money, and any additional income was a godsend to her, anyway. So in June 1953, I started to take weekly half-hour English lessons. As with everything else, my parents encouraged me, especially on hearing promising reports from Auntie Mici about my ability in languages. I bless the moment of that decision and thank God every day for the enlightenment that spurred me on to study English despite all the obstacles.

During these difficult times my parents seemed to fight a lot, mostly over money, or, I should say, over the lack of it. I hated it when they fought. When people love each other, nothing should be important enough to fight over, I thought, and I resolved never to fight with my husband when I was married, no matter what. Because of the congenital heart condition that first surfaced when she was in her early twenties, my mother's health was also steadily deteriorating. She had a good job as a bookkeeper, but she often had to take time off for sick leave (with reduced pay) to gain back some of her strength. My father worked long hours but did not seem to be able to substantially improve his financial standing at his place of employment in the toy factory, even though eventually he was promoted to foreman.

My parents' recreation consisted of visits from friends in the evenings or weekends to play cards. Occasionally they would meet with friends at one of the city's many coffee houses for an espresso to discuss the children, work, or politics, always in hushed tones. They would go on outings to Margaret Island, and my father would sometimes attend a soccer game with his friends on Sunday afternoons. Trips or vacations, however, were out of the question.

In the summer, we were required to work full time for four weeks as part of our studies at the Technikum. We were given internship positions at related industrial sites and acquired practical experience while earning a small salary. My brother and I also continued with occasional employment at the National

Sports Stadium, selling pretzels, candy, and refreshments in the stands during soccer games and other athletic events.

During the winter, after heavy snowfalls, we joined street crews to shovel the snow from the sidewalks and tram tracks for a small hourly wage. I wasn't very strong, so after a few attempts, I was told not to bother going back, but my brother went a lot, and, from what I understand, he bitterly resented having to do so. He preferred to work for his friend, Laci's father, Béla bácsi, who was a well-respected electrical contractor and head of one of the few cooperatives allowed to function under strict government guidelines. Regardless of where we worked, we were expected to hand over all our earnings to our parents for family expenses. We received a small weekly allowance. I suspected that somehow Johnny managed to outmaneuver our parents, for he always seemed to have a lot more money at his disposal than I did.

Soon after my fifteenth birthday, I met Peter, my first serious boyfriend, at the National Sports Stadium after a soccer match. We were both working the stands and our paths crossed in the crowd as we were returning our trays, mine laden with pretzels and candy, his with refreshments and beer. We both stopped in our tracks, and as we looked at each other the world around us truly ceased to exist. I can still see him standing there under the concrete bleachers with his blonde, wavy hair, deep blue eyes, and his endearing, funny smile that hardly ever left his face. "Pardon me," he called out, "may I buy a pretzel from you? I am hungry, and I would like to get to know you." He handed me a large bill and watched closely as I counted out the change. Later that afternoon, I managed to "lose" my brother (who unofficially was in charge of my safety) and let Peter walk me home. To my great surprise at one point, I even let him hold my hand, and then I further let him kiss me good night on the lips as we parted. I guess I was smitten, but, in addition, I was absolutely confused. I was elated about my experience with Peter, but at the same time, I felt guilty about it. I had been told repeatedly over the years that "nice girls" don't let boys pick them up on the street, they don't hold hands at least until the fifth date, and most definitely they don't let a boy kiss them for months, and even then never on the lips.

Peter Z. was a first-year mechanical engineering student at the Technical University of Budapest. He took his studies very seriously. He lived with his widowed mother in a small apartment on the Buda side of the city. We were both poor, so our infrequent dates consisted of him visiting me at home. My parents liked him and didn't mind his presence, as long as the door of the room was wide open. We would play chess or cards or we would help each other with homework. He helped me with my math and physics projects, while I was able to assist him with technical drawing and descriptive geometry assignments. He played the piano well, so we would learn and play four-hand pieces together. Sometimes, weather permitting, we went for long walks, strolling arm in arm along the banks of the Danube River or on Margaret Island, occasionally stealing a kiss in secluded spots. We talked a lot. I was able to have meaningful discussions with him on many topics, including classical music and politics. He had a great sense of humor that transcended the gloom and doom of our existence, so we laughed and were happy when we were together. I felt sure he understood me as a person. He understood my hopes and my dreams, and he listened to my opinion and seemed to respect it. I considered him a true soul mate and thought he was the most wonderful person I had ever met in my life. He was highly intelligent, with a gentle soul in his muscular, swimmer's body developed through years of water-polo matches. I fell deeply in love in no time at all.

One day, I was able to get inexpensive group tickets at the Operetta House to see Franz Lehár's "The Count of Luxemburg" (*Luxemburg Grófja*). A week earlier, on our sixth-month anniversary, Peter had told me that the evening would have to be our last date. According to his mother, I was proving to be too much of a distraction for him. I took him away from his studies, and he had to concur. That evening, during the performance on stage, the heroine sang her good byes to the hero " *No, my Sir, the rainbow is far, you can't get there by wings of desire. It is better if we don't see each other, … we have no hope for happiness together.*" Meanwhile high up in the balcony, to the strains of Lehár's romantic, lovely words and music, Peter kissed me good-bye and I knew there was no use in objecting. I tried hard to accept his decision and my disappointment with grace. Breaking up was very difficult for me. I put away his letters and his photograph and buried my memories with his picture in a small corner of my heart, reminding myself that I still had my pride, my family and friends, my studies, and, above all, my dreams.

After this painful breakup with Peter, I avoided going out for fear of getting involved in another relationship and possibly getting hurt again. At this time, my life was filled with schoolwork, piano practice, and studying.

Throughout these years, in the winter, I would visit the neighborhood skating rink with friends, renting skates by the hour. Most of the time I would meet my childhood friend, Viktor, who was an excellent skater, and he would guide me through some dance steps to the music, holding me like a true ice dancer. I still longed to own a pair of skates and learn to skate like Sonja Henie, but by the time I turned sixteen, I was realistic enough to know that it was not to be, especially after I fell on a simple waltz jump. As I walked the three blocks home that night, my ankle hurt so much that I realized it must be more than a sprain. For two weeks I hid my pain, not displaying even a slight limp in the presence of my parents, because I was afraid of their reaction about the expense of an accidental medical problem. At night, I would wait until everybody was asleep, then put cold compresses on my ankle, waiting for the pain to subside, so I could go to sleep. This went on until Auntie Balázs noticed me limping in school and gave me an ultimatum: I had to tell my parents or she would show up for a visit and tell them. Now my parents had two reasons to be angry with me, first, the expense, and then the fact that I had deceived them. After taking an x-ray of my ankle, the doctor could not believe that I managed to walk on a broken ankle for two weeks without limping. He promptly put my leg in a cast for eight frustrating weeks.

Fortunately, I loved sitting at the window of our room, listening to music while I read, knitted, or crocheted and dreamt about the future, which made the time go faster while I recuperated. I tried to keep up with my knitting and crocheting, alternating between several projects. Auntie Maria still visited my parents occasionally, and she would bring me patterns and teach me more complicated stitches and designs. While my hands were busy, I would daydream, visualizing myself being married with two or three children, working as a respected scientist or mathematician, and living in a nice home with no financial worries.

From an early age on, I loved to read, especially books of history and travel. I imagined myself being able to travel all over the world, visiting famous cities like Washington, New York, Montreal, Paris, London, Rome, and Vienna, and seeing famous sights like Niagara Falls, and the Great Wall of China, places I read about in my books. Seeing that my head was in the clouds, my parents made sure that my feet were firmly planted on the ground. They expected their children to be aware of their environment, to cope with daily challenges, and also to help others in need.

Despite the displacement of many "undesirable" families to the countryside, there was a tremendous shortage of apartments in Budapest. On one side of our apartment house, in the attic above the top floor, there was a communal laundry area, which was seldom used. A young couple found out about it, laid claim to it, and had it converted into a tiny one-bedroom apartment.

They were very poor. He was a construction worker, while she found employment nearby as a manicurist. Auntie Mariska took the young, inexperienced, nineteen-year-old bride, Csöppi, under her wing and I also became her friend, especially when I found out that she was expecting a child. By the time the baby was born, we were so close that she asked me to become the godmother of her newborn baby girl, Zsuzsa. I accepted happily and doted on the beautiful little girl. I spent a lot of time playing with her and babysitting. Both of her parents were strong, healthy, and good-looking, and she inherited an angelic face from her mother, with a radiant smile, deep brown eyes, and olive skin, with finely chiseled features, and from her father, a muscular, well-proportioned body. When she got a little bigger, around two years old, she would wait for me by the railing in front of her door and start screaming with delight, "Ulika, Ulika, come see Zsuzsa," as she spotted me walking through the swinging doors on my way home from school. We got to love each other, Csöppi, her husband, Jóska, and their daughter, Zsuzsa, with a love that survived years of separation.

Another friend, Lia, my best friend during my Technikum years, lived a few blocks from us, next to St Stephen's Park. We would commute to school together every day. We had known each other in elementary school, where we attended the same classes, but we were not close until we found each other in the same classes at the Technikum again. She was very outgoing and kept bugging me to go with her to different high school or university dances.

One day in the spring of 1954, she pressured me into accompanying her to a dance at the technical university. "Maybe you will bump into Peter," she told me, "or who knows, you might bump into something better." I was skeptical on both counts; I knew Peter wouldn't be there and I was not interested in the "anything better" I might bump into, either. However, I eventually gave in and went along, especially since Johnny and his two friends, Laci and Gömbi, wanted to join us. Most of the time I had fun with them and I could always stay out a little later when I went out in the company of my brother.

The large ballroom was crowded, with a small, live, jazz band on a podium against one wall playing American style dance music. Of course, as I expected, Peter wasn't there. But there in the crowd I saw another handsome young man. He looked a lot like Peter, but was much taller, with brown instead of blue eyes, and without his endearing smile. He asked me to dance. Rezső C., as he introduced himself, was a second year electronics-engineering student at the technical university. He kept returning throughout the evening to ask me to dance again and again. He danced very well, his lean, muscular body swaying in perfect rhythm with the music. It was easy to tell that he was musical and that he was enjoying himself. At times, he would send his friends, Iván Sós or Robert Bán, to dance with me and by the way they were talking, I could tell they were "checking me out." Rezső was a well-dressed, sharp-looking fellow with straight blonde hair and expressive, deep brown eyes. He talked a lot and turned out to be highly intelligent (a trait that seemed very important to me) as well as good looking. By the time he asked me for a date, I was pretty impressed with his intellect, as well as with his looks, and I agreed to meet him downtown for an espresso the following Saturday. The whole week, I kept wondering if I should keep our date and (on the other hand) if he was going to show up. When the day came, we both were there, although he was more than fashionably late, a habit of his, that he broke only once in his life. He was on time— no, actually he was early, for our wedding two and a half years later.

My junior year passed quickly. By the time I started my senior year at the BV Technikum in the fall of 1954, life was quite full. I was careful to keep up my grades, for the next hurdle of my life was approaching, trying to find a good position in Budapest after graduation, rather than in a smaller city in the country where most of the job openings were.

I no longer considered applying to the university. My parents made it pretty clear that, "If anybody in this family goes to University, that's going to be your brother." As an explanation, they added, "Not that he has the grades for it, but certainly he has the smarts and, anyway, it is more important for a boy to get a good education." Although I felt deeply resentful of their justification for this decision, I accepted it. Besides, by this time I had had enough of hardships and was fed up with being poor. Now I had my heart set on finding a good job, one that I would like, preferably one that would also pay well, so I could start saving for a better future, one that I felt would include children as well.

I was truly excited about my chosen career. I was hoping to find a position as an engineering draftsman in a consulting engineering office. My teachers had assured me that, despite the slight tremor in my hands, my work was of very high quality, regardless of whether I worked with ink or pencil. Early on, I was able to devise several techniques to compensate for the affliction, so all my lines were crisp and precise, my lettering uniform, without the slightest sign of wavering. I was confident too that my calculations and layouts were correct, thanks to my mathematical skills, my spatial sense, and my knowledge of building codes and materials. I put together a portfolio and waited for job openings to be posted while I was preparing for the much-dreaded state final high school exit exams.

By this time, our homeroom of twenty-five students had jelled together into a group of friends. I think this was largely due to the talents of our class president, Iván Wolf, and the gentle loving leadership of our teacher, Auntie Balázs. She told us repeatedly that she thought we were an unusually gifted group of students and even though most of us opted for jobs after graduation, she kept predicting an eventual university degree and a bright future for us all. At the time we didn't believe her, but years later, when she presided over our twenty-fifth class reunion, we realized how right she had been. We counted twenty-five bachelor degrees, several masters, and even two doctorates among us. At the next class reunion, our thirty-fifth, Auntie Balázs proudly produced a map of the world on which she had marked all the diverse locations in Europe, Africa, Australia, and North and South America of the universities where these diplomas originated.

The graduation dance for all three graduating classes that year was to be held in the school's decorated gymnasium. We were not expected to wear formal gowns, just nice dresses for the girls and suits with ties for the boys. Trouble was, I didn't have a suitable nice dress, and neither did we have the money to buy one. I was faced with two choices: the first was not to go to the graduation dance, and the second was to sell my beloved, beautiful Katie doll and use the money for a combined dance and graduation dress. With a heavy heart, I parted with my cherished Katie and gave her up for adoption, expecting one day to buy her back for my own little girl. Sadly, I never could get Katie back, nor did I ever have a daughter who would have appreciated her.

My father bought a royal blue light wool material for my graduation dress and Aunt Manci, his sister-in-law, who was an accomplished seamstress and designer, made a fashionable one-of-a-kind dress for me. I wore it to the dance with a scarf, to graduation with the school pin, and to job interviews with a thin gold necklace that belonged to my mother. Being dressed just right for the occasion was important to me. It made me feel pretty and gave me self-confidence.

I studied very hard for the final exit exams, especially mathematics, for I felt I had something to prove to myself and to my beloved teacher, *Spugyi bácsi*. When the final grades were in, I was pleased with the results. Most importantly, I earned an honorable mention in mathematics from the panel of examiners and had A's in all the subjects that were important for me to get the job I was hoping for. I received a pleasant surprise from *Spugyi bácsi,* who presented me with a handbook of mathematical tables bearing his inscription. "There is no royal road. With best wishes from your teacher, Imre Pálos." Best of all, on hearing the results, my father patted me on the head with obvious pride, calling me *kis okos,* his rare recognition to me for a job well done.

On the evening of the graduation dance, Auntie Mariska made a festive dinner. Rezső, to whom I had grown close since we had met at the university dance in the spring a year earlier, showed up almost on time with a corsage. The two of us, together with Johnny and his date, and my friend Lia and her date, took the tramway to the school for our graduation dance. We had a good time celebrating. When a number of us missed the last tramway for the night, we ended up with a two-hour walk home.

Ordinarily, when I went out in the evenings, I had to be home by eleven o'clock, which was when the superintendent of the building locked the front door to the apartment house. This was the custom of the times. Any tenant coming home after eleven had to ring for the superintendent and pay a small fee for the front door to be unlocked. Fortunately, my brother and I did not have to keep to the curfew the night of our graduation dance; we had permission from our parents to stay out until after the dance was over at midnight, but we were supposed to stay together.

On our way home, we passed a construction site with a pile of red bricks on the sidewalk next to the entrance of a building. Somebody had the bright idea, that we should transfer the bricks to the sidewalk on the other side of the street. We quickly formed a chain across the street and quietly and carefully, brick by brick, moved the whole pile to the opposite side, then continued on our way home. We had great fun imagining the faces of the construction workers the next morning as they discovered their bricks neatly piled on the other side of the street from where they had left them the day before.

Before falling asleep with the memories of a nice evening, I resolved that one day, when I had something to celebrate again, I would be prosperous enough to be able to afford a taxi ride to Margaret Island and have dinner in the fine restaurant at the elegant Grand Hotel. Happy as I was with my lot that night, I promised myself something better for the future.

When the job openings were finally posted, I applied and interviewed for several of them. On all the application forms I had to complete there was a question where you had to mark your ancestry from among the choices listed as "proletariat," "peasant," "intellectual," or the dreaded "class outsider." However, what employers seemed to be really interested in were my grades and my skills. To my great relief, I realized that at this point it seemed that nobody was unduly interested in my social status any more. I had no trouble getting the job I wanted as an electrical design draftsman with a decent salary at the Könnyüi-pari Tervező Iroda, a consulting engineering firm in downtown Budapest.

Johnny took a position as a maintenance electrician in a power plant in Dörög, a small city located a three-hour bus ride from the capital. When I teased him about exchanging his snow shovel for a coal shovel, he just laughed. I think he could have found a job in Budapest, but he wanted to move away from home and be independent. My parents were disappointed and Auntie Mariska was heartbroken, but Johnny insisted that this was a good career move for him and they reluctantly accepted his decision. While I missed him, I was happy to have our room to myself.

The plant where my brother worked was an old, coal-fired, power plant. To his dismay, he soon discovered that the place was hot everywhere, and coal dust covered everything. "I never realized how many diverse electrical parts can go wrong in an old power plant," he complained. Being independent did not turn out to be as great as my brother had imagined. Living in a strange city, in a small room, having to take care of his every need himself was not quite the good life he envisioned. Above all, I think Johnny missed Auntie Mariska's cooking and splendid pastries. Within months, he had had enough. He gave up his independence, found a position through a classmate in another power plant in Kispest, an industrial suburb of Budapest, and moved back home. "There goes my private room," I complained, half jokingly, but deep down I liked having him around.

I was pleased with the turn of events in my life and considered myself extremely lucky. I remembered the words of Immanuel Kant: "There are three essential ingredients for happiness; Something to Love, Something to Do, and Something to Hope for". It seemed that, all of a sudden, after years of uncertainty and hardship, I finally had them all and I was happy.

On the left, Julie's Grandfather Ferenc and Grandmother Anna Adler, in the middle, her Uncle Nándi and Aunt Manci, on the right Julie's father Zsigmond and her mother Katalin around 1935

The twins, Johnny and Julie (*Jancsi és Juliska*)
with their parents on Margaret Island in 1940

The four year old twins on Margaret Island in 1941

The twins in 1947

The twins in 1951

The seventh-grade class of the *Sziget* Street Elementary School in 1950. Julie is seated in the front row, third from the left, her friend Susie is the seventh from the left in the middle row. Her other friend Lia is the sixth girl from the left in the top row, while Clara is the first.

The graduating class of the Budapesti Villamosenergiaipari Technikum in 1955. Julie is the first from the left in the third row, while Johnny is the third in the fourth row. Julie's friend Lia is the fifth from the right in the third row. Class President Iván Wolf is first from the right in the bottom row. School Principal, Dénes Takács is in top row center. Homeroom teacher Auntie Balázs is in third row center, while Julie's beloved *Spugyi bácsi* (Imre Pálos) is the third from the right in the second row.

Julie's high school graduation picture (1955)

Julie and Rezsö during a mountain excursion in the summer of 1956

Chapter Six

GAINFUL EMPLOYMENT AT LAST

In 1953, after Stalin's death and during the Twentieth Congress of the Soviet Communist Party, another former Hungarian communist exile with Rákosi in Moscow, Imre Nagy, became Prime Minister of Hungary, while Rákosi hung on to power by maintaining his influential position as First Secretary of the Communist Party. News of changes in the Soviet governing hierarchy prompted the communist government in Hungary to promise much needed reforms. As the two factions, Imre Nagy and the so-called reform communists on one side, and Mátyás Rákosi and his hard liners on the other, struggled for power, very few of the promised improvements in the political and economic life of Hungary were implemented. Life for the average citizen remained difficult both in the cities and the countryside, with living standards remaining at the subsistence level for the majority of Hungarians.

Immediately after my graduation from the Electrical Engineering Gymnasium High School (KKV Technikum) in 1955, I started my first job as a draftsman at the Könnyűipari Tervező Iroda consulting engineering firm. The office had about 150 employees working on all aspects of project design related to light industrial manufacturing companies, offices, hospitals, and medical buildings. I was content and considered myself fortunate to have an interesting, steady job where I could use my education, while having prospects for advancement to a more challenging position in design work.

Luckily, all the draftsmen (and ladies, of course) were required to wear white lab coats over their street clothes, so being fashionably attired did not present a financial problem. One could wear almost anything—or on warm days almost nothing—under the lab coats, which made life much more bearable without air-conditioners on hot summer days.

On the first day I reported to work, I was assigned the basic tools and my very own drafting table, which was located on the second floor of the building towards the middle of a huge corner room. The desirable tables, which were allocated by seniority, were located by the large bay windows facing the street corner on two sides. At those choice positions the lighting was better and nobody was walking behind you or, worse, bumping into your chair and disturbing your concentration. I resolved that one day I would earn the right to have one of those choice drafting tables by a window. Near the entrance to the large hall, the design engineers had their own desks and drafting tables in spacious individual cubicles behind shoulder-height frosted glass partitions. Occasionally, I would even get carried away and dream that maybe, with time, I could take evening courses at the Technical University and graduate to an engineering cubicle.

As I found out soon enough, the equipment we were issued was of inferior quality, so I, like others, ended up having to buy my own higher quality tools. These were usually imported from Germany and sometimes available only on the black market. I got permission from my parents to allocate some money from my monthly paycheck for the equipment I needed: different sized acrylic triangles, precision scale measuring rulers, mechanical pencils, sharpeners, erasers, a grand compass set, and a large, good-quality slide rule. With all that first class equipment at my fingertips, I felt prosperous and important, and I signed my name with pride to each of my drawings. I found the work very enjoyable while challenging.

My immediate supervisor, a smart, pretty, young woman named Györgyi, and I hit it off right away. We got along very well both professionally and personally. She seemed to be happy all the time, with a constant smile on her round face and a permanent twinkle in her big brown eyes. She liked to joke around, but she took her work very seriously, expecting perfection from herself as well as from her associates. I rapidly grew to respect her knowledge and professionalism.

Our department worked on lighting and power distribution designs for small factories, offices, and medical buildings that were either new or needed upgrading as part of renovations. Györgyi would receive general instructions directly from the architect and design engineer. Then she would work out the details, write specifications, and advise me on how to represent the layout on drawings that would be given to the workers and tradesmen at the construction site. Under these circumstances, my spatial sense, combined with a good sense of direction, served me very well. After examining a set of drawings, I could see the whole building in my mind's eye and move around in it as if I had spent time there. This was an ability that was extremely valuable, especially when dealing with new designs.

Within six months, Györgyi started giving me assignments that carried some design responsibility and arranged for me to get the drafting table next to hers, closer to the window. I now occupied the second table away from the window. What a promotion! The move was an obvious sign of recognition; in my eyes, it was better than a raise, although a modest raise did follow later.

I realized that in order to receive a substantial raise it was not enough to do my work in an exceptional manner. I would have to behave more politically correctly and apply for membership in the DISZ (the communist youth organization), attend meetings after work and contribute constructively to the discussions on the "superiority of the Marxist-Leninist ideology over the capitalist system." However, my logical mind and common sense revolted against the endless communist propaganda we were fed. It simply did not make sense to me. Of course, questioning the prevailing party line openly at these meetings would have been suicidal. The only acceptable action would have been to continue with deception and extol the virtues of communism, which I could not bring myself to do. For me, the economic advantages to toeing the party line were not worth the price of compromising what I considered to be my integrity. Like most of my friends, I could only take part in these activities with the minimum time and effort necessary to keep my job.

Much as I liked Györgyi, there appeared to be a nagging obstacle to being her true friend. Shortly after our first meeting, when she casually mentioned that her husband was the secretary of the Communist Party cell at his workplace, I realized that I had to think about every word I said to her and watch how I said it. Discussing my background was not wise, while any remark, no matter how innocent, relating to politics was out of the question. Deep down, I did not think she would betray me, but I valued my job far too much to take a chance, so I was always on my guard with her regardless of the topic for discussion. Later, when I got to know her better, I realized that she had informed me of her husband's position as a kind of warning in order to avoid politically unwise discussions, and forestall complications in our relationship.

At lunchtime, during this period of my life, I often visited the historic Franciscan Catholic Church a couple of blocks from the office. I always made sure nobody saw me enter. Sitting at the exact spot where Franz Liszt, the famous Hungarian composer, had spent his later years in prayer and meditation, I would thank God for helping me achieve some of my dreams and pray for His continued support. Most of the time, somebody would be practicing on the magnificent pipe organ, and the sounds filled my soul with music and peace. These moments helped me immensely in keeping a sense of hope for a better future despite economic hardships and the limitations imposed on me by the oppressive environment of a communist dominated society.

One day, I saw a familiar figure on her knees at a side altar. She had a black scarf on her head and was fervently praying, oblivious to her surroundings. I could tell she was distraught and sobbing. Pretending not to have seen her, I rushed out of the church and back to the office. Most desks were still without their occupants, including Györgyi's. When the woman I'd seen came back from lunch, her eyes were red. She complained of a headache and left for home, taking the afternoon off. I never told her that I had seen her in church, even after she confided in me that her hopes for a baby had been dashed again for the umpteenth time that morning. I could not help wondering if her communist husband knew where his wife had spent her lunchtime that day, and I noted with relief, that for the human soul, communist ideology was no match for the word of God.

My life at home at this time was not nearly as smooth as it might have seemed to a casual observer. I loved and appreciated my parents, who, despite their difficult lives, were able to maintain an atmosphere of affection and caring in our home. I also respected them for their strength in the face of adversity and for who they were, for their humanity. My mother, a business gymnasium graduate with years of experience as a bookkeeper, was clever and astute, with a talent for music and literature. My father, a smart, self-educated man, had an indomitable spirit. He was sociable, outgoing, and the whole world was his friend. Although years of hardship had left their marks on both my parents, they aged gracefully, and together they were still a strikingly handsome couple. It was touching to see how my father spoiled my mother and how my reserved mother enjoyed his gregarious nature.

My father always took a special interest in my brother's friends, especially those whose fathers had not returned from the war or concentration camps. Meeting them on the street, he would invite them to our place and inquire about their school-work, sports, girlfriends, hopes, and dreams. This was greatly appreciated by the boys, and even more by their mothers, who often sought his advice on family matters.

My parents loved children, but above all, they were dedicated to the welfare of their own twins, whom they considered to be their pride and joy. Being bombarded daily by propaganda they knew to be lies had to be frustrating for them. Working long hours for inadequate pay, constantly worrying about short-age of money, medicine, food—just trying to make ends meet— had made living exhausting for them. I still marvel at their forti-tude. It must have been very hard, trying to live life to the fullest under those difficult circumstances.

Unfortunately for me, however, they seemed to have been unable to adjust to the fact that their little girl had matured and was becoming a young woman. My parents and Auntie Mariska still treated me like a child. They had a hard time accepting the fact that I needed space of my own, especially since at work I was gaining respect as a mature, up-and-coming professional. "When you are in your own house, my dear, you can have your own rules. As long as you are in ours, you have to abide by ours," was the standard response to my attempts to gain some independence. I resented having to account to my parents for all my actions, but above all, I hated the fact that their "inquisition" forced me into an occasional lie, rather than risk disapproval, lengthy lectures, or even punishment.

Another source of resentment was the fact that I had to hand over my entire paycheck to my parents for "room and board," receiving a small amount for transportation, lunch, and "pocket money." I did not think this was fair at all, but my mother's health was poor and I did not want to upset her, so I didn't ob-ject too vigorously. Each time I tried to discuss my finances, she would get highly agitated, lamenting that her selfish children did not appreciate the sacrifices she had made for them throughout her life, so I would give up. According to my mother's own often repeated diagnosis, the root cause of her heart condition was attributable to carrying twins during her pregnancy and the difficulty of the multiple birth. This placed a heavy burden of guilt on Johnny's and my shoulders. All through our childhood, every time we did something against our mother's wishes, she would accuse us of being selfish, cold-hearted and ruthless, of "pushing her one step closer to her grave" by upsetting her. There was no denying that she had a congenital heart condition, yet as I grew older, I began to suspect that she was using her frail health as a weapon to get her way in family disputes. Nevertheless, I gave in to her wishes, as we all did, which reinforced her behavior.

The constant financial hardship and insecurity of our formative years left its mark on Johnny and me for the rest of our lives, though in different ways. My father used to emphasize that "money does not bring happiness, and, besides you can't take it with you," even though he was frugal and from his meager income saved as much money as he could all his life. His recipe for happiness was his belief that material possessions enslave you, but your intellect and your heart set you free. Although he is prudent, my brother is very generous with himself and with others, while I am constantly saving, being afraid of the poverty tomorrow might bring. Yet neither of us is materialistic. We both are still learning about balancing saving and spending habits.

Being without any funds of my own while earning a steady income was extremely frustrating and depressing. I decided to open a secret bank account, where every week I deposited half of my lunch money, making do with the other half. In addition, I was able to save a little from occasional overtime work, a fact I managed to keep from my parents. Even the small amounts I was able to set aside this way seemed to give me a sense of security and some hope for the future of financial freedom I so desperately craved. Having a good job with a steady income and my own private savings account boosted my self-esteem and self-confidence.

During the summer, on Sundays (I worked regular hours on Saturdays, from eight to two), Rezsö and I would go on excursions to the Danube Bend, north of the city, where we would rent a kayak and swim. The government and company-sponsored sports clubs owned the boathouses along the river that gave no access for ordinary citizens. Luckily, we had access to one of the clubhouses and its boats, as in his youth Rezsö had pursued boating seriously as a sport. One year, he had been Hungarian doubles kayak champion with his friend, Iván Sós.

I liked being near water, but Rezsö preferred the mountains. Naturally, we compromised and often would go to the mountains. For a day-long excursion, we would meet early in the morning at the cog railway station at the foot of Freedom Mountain *(Szabadsághegy)*, not far from his home on the Buda side. It would take me a forty-five minute ride on the streetcar to meet him there. Then we would sit on wooden benches in the red carriages as the old train slowly made its way up the hill, guided on its tracks by a central cogged wheel. Once on the top, we would walk, and talk, enjoying the fresh, pure mountain air. Nearby, there was another sightseeing rail line, the *Úttörö Vasút*, run by the Young Communist Pioneer organization, with youngsters operating the entire business, except for driving the steam engines.

Occasionally, we would take a day trip with friends by train to Lake Balaton, the "landlocked sea of Hungary," or to a smaller, less developed lake called Lake Velence, which was closer. Sometimes we would go out on Saturday night with a group of friends, or by ourselves, to one of the many coffeehouses around Budapest, where usually a small ensemble played live music and there was a small dance floor. When we were alone, we would find a table, order an espresso with a small sandwich or pastry (neither of us liked alcoholic beverages), and hold hands and talk. I loved to dance, and so did Rezsö, especially when I let him hold me close during slow numbers. We both would softly sing along with the familiar *chansons*, slowly swaying to the music, while time flew. By now, we had an exclusive relationship and we were definitely attracted to each other. Our hormones were raging and sparks were flying.

My parents were not thrilled. They thought I was too young to get involved in a serious relationship. They wanted me to go out with different young men before I committed myself. In addition, my mother had a friend whose son, Michael, tried without success to court me, although he was persistent and she encouraged the relationship. "He is a good man, and he adores you," my mother would tell me. "He would treat you like gold for the rest of your life." However, the poor guy didn't have a chance with me, as he was short and pudgy, not good looking at all, and being a certified accountant, he was not interested in the sciences, nor in music. Worst of all he was a DISZ (communist youth organization) member being groomed for Communist Party membership. In contrast, Rezsö was an electrical engineering student at the Technical University. He was tall and muscular, with fine features, and I could talk freely about topics of interest to me: my job, his studies, physics, history, music, and even politics.

Despite my sentiments, or perhaps because of them, I don't think my mother ever liked Rezsö as a person, while my father seemed neutral. I especially remember a long discussion my mother and I once had, during which she advised me against ever marrying Rezsö because she thought he was conceited, self-centered, and controlling. Of course, I didn't see any of that. I thought Rezsö had a strong character, while I believed what she called his conceit was self-confidence, his "self-centered" traits were a manifestation of his superior intellect, and his "controlling" was due to jealousy born of his love for me. I thought

Rezsö was handsome, smart, witty, and multitalented, for, in addition to his obvious expertise in the sciences, he loved music and played the piano beautifully. Why, he could even play melodies by ear, and then improvise and harmonize as he went along, something I never had the talent for. I realized that, slowly, I was falling in love again, despite objections from that little corner of my heart, where the image of Peter, my first love, seemed to have permanent residence.

Rezsö also had a dry sense of humor, which was entertaining at times, but would occasionally lead him into making careless, insensitive, hurtful remarks that would bother me for days. When I complained, he would tell me that the problem was with me, because I didn't have a sense of humor or I was insecure, too sensitive. Deep down, I knew I was not, although at times I began to wonder. I had a loving family, many friends, and a secure professional life, yet I started accepting the blame for the emotional distress I experienced as a result of his treatment of me. Occasionally I could not help but wonder if he was putting me down on purpose, but for what purpose? I could not imagine a reason why he would do that, especially if he loved me, as he said he did. Unfortunately, I had nobody with whom I felt comfortable to discuss my concerns, so I just brushed them aside.

There was one thing, though, that I intensely disliked about Rezsö. He was a very heavy smoker. Knowing how I felt, he cut back considerably, especially when we were together. He claimed that being with me made him forget his problems and his cigarettes, but when we were apart, he needed to smoke to help him cope with his life. He said he needed the cigarettes to quiet his anxiety about excelling at the university and promised to quit after graduation. Despite my intuition telling me otherwise, I chose to believe Rezsö's promise to quit and put up with his habit, even though I hated it.

Most young people were smoking at the time, but I never tried it myself, as I considered it a disgusting habit in addition to being an unnecessary expense. Auntie Mariska was also a very heavy smoker all her life, until her doctor put an end to it during a medical check-up, when he found that her blood pressure was extremely high. At the age of sixty, she was told by the doctor to choose between not smoking or the probability of a sudden death within three months. She quit cold turkey from one day to the next, and I was delighted for her. My mother never smoked, but my father would have an occasional cigarette and eventually so would my brother. Both of Rezsö's parents and his brother were heavy smokers.

My mother warmed up to Rezsö a little bit after he successfully repaired our radio a couple of times, and for free at that. He would show up with his small tool chest, change the vacuum tubes, fix the dials, thoroughly impressing her with his know-how. Even Auntie Mariska was amazed when, on one occasion, she watched him turn a silent box full of wires and tubes into a resonating source of beautiful music. To my great surprise, she invited him to stay for dinner that Sunday night, the ultimate sign of acceptance from her.

Since his early high school days, Rezsö had experimented with electricity and radios, taking them apart, then fixing and reassembling them. He became so proficient that he was able to make money on the side by repairing radios for relatives, friends, and neighbors. As his repair work expanded, however, his mother became very upset. What if somebody were to report him and his illegal repair business? He would most certainly be expelled from the university and might even be put into jail.

Rezsö's mother, Elsa Mama, as we called her, was a devout Catholic and raised her two boys, Gyuri and Rezsö, as Catholics. I don't think she disliked me personally, but I know she wasn't thrilled about her son getting seriously involved with a girl of Jewish background. Interestingly enough, though, both of Rezsö's best friends, Iván Sós and Robie Bán, were Jewish, and she loved them both, so maybe that wasn't her sole reason for being cool toward me.

Perhaps her objections originated from a somewhat snobbish attitude: because I did not come from a scholarly family. While Rezsö, senior, held a university diploma, my father didn't even have a high school one. Rezsö's brother, Gyuri, was also a university graduate with a business degree, while my brother and I had only high school diplomas. It didn't seem to make any difference to her that, despite a lack of formal education, our family led an intellectually rich life filled with books and music. I believe, for her, I was still "just stupid little Julie from the other side of the tracks," an attitude that her son seemed to have sometimes adopted, especially when he felt the emotional need or when it served his purpose during a dispute.

Elsa Mama's best friend had a daughter, Marika, who was Catholic and a freshman-engineering student at the technical university. Elsa Mama made no secret of the fact that she would have preferred Marika as a prospective daughter-in-law, but neither Rezsö, nor Marika seemed the least bit interested.

In her younger days, Elsa Mama had been employed as an executive assistant, although she did not work outside the home after the birth of her first child, Gyuri. Rezsö's father held down two full-time jobs to support the family.

For years and years, Rezsö, senior, worked as a high school business teacher from eight till two o'clock in the afternoon. After a short nap, he headed for another full time job from 5 P.M. till 2 A.M. at the Hungarian News Agency, monitoring, translating, and transcribing foreign newscasts in French and German. Except for his summer vacation time from school, he kept up this grueling schedule for fourteen years. To make sure there were jobs open in support of the communists' claim of zero percent unemployment, it was against the law for citizens to hold down two full-time jobs. Yet somehow Rezsö, senior, found a way to do it without getting reported or found out by the authorities. The feat must have been really difficult to accomplish, for according to the law he was responsible for supplying both employers with a single-issue "work permit record book." He continued this grueling pace till his retirement from both jobs in 1962. Tragically, not long after, he died suddenly from a massive heart attack.

While I only met Rezsö, senior, a few times, I felt at ease with him when we were together. Having been a high school teacher, he understood young people. He seemed to be interested in me and my hopes and dreams. I believe that we took an instant liking to each other that lasted throughout the years.

Although I was working full time after my graduation in 1955, when September rolled around it was strange not to have to go to school, and I missed it. However, I still had my weekly piano and English lessons and I studied diligently. By now I could read English fairly well with the aid of a dictionary and could write short compositions. However, my conversational skills were extremely poor, for outside of my lessons with my teacher, I had nobody to practice with. Listening to foreign language broadcasts from Western Europe was arduous, since the communist government was making reception difficult by jamming these programs continuously. Nevertheless, I liked the idea of being able to understand and communicate in another tongue, so I persevered.

In the spring of 1956, with encouragement from Auntie Mici, my language teacher, I also started learning German, which seemed easier because my parents spoke German fluently. As a matter of fact, ever since I remember, they would switch to German when they wanted to say something to each other without us children understanding what they were talking about. One of them would start with *Nicht fur die kinder*, meaning "not for the children," a definite signal for us to start listening really hard. Sure enough, through some strange process, I began to understand intuitively the essence of their conversation. So when I started my German lessons, the language was not completely foreign to me. I could also talk with my parents a little bit, which made it more interesting.

In March I celebrated my last birthday as a teenager. I turned nineteen. In the office, I was recognized as a responsible, reliable worker and I received respect, while at home I was still treated as a little girl with very little personal and financial freedom granted by my strict parents. My brother had many more privileges, like later curfews, more money, and much less scrutiny, because "boys needed more space." I began to begrudge my lack of personal freedom. I was becoming increasingly more frustrated and resentful. Each time I questioned an inequity, I was told by my parents, that my brother was a guy and I was a girl, and this is how life had to be as long as I was living under their roof. "When you are in your own home, my dear, you can do as you wish, but while you live here, you have to abide by our rules." It surprised me greatly that my sensible father would be so inflexible and unreasonable, but it was clear from his attitude that in his house he would let nobody defy his rules, and that was that.

One incident that stands out as a defining moment in my teenage existence had unfortunate consequences to my relationship with my parents for the rest of my life. Rezsö and I went out with a few friends on a Saturday evening in May to celebrate his twenty-second birthday with dinner at a small restaurant that had musicians and a small dance floor. As usual, I was expected to be home before eleven o'clock, when, according to custom, the building superintendent locked the main door to the entrance of our apartment building. I made a conscious decision not to go home before midnight. After all, I had enough money of my own to pay the required fee to have the front door to the building unlocked, and I felt that at nineteen, I was old enough to stay out till midnight like my brother and our friends.

The evening was also notable for another special reason. Following a pleasant dinner and some dancing, Rezsö and I walked along the banks of the Danube River and talked about the future. It was a beautiful, clear, spring night, unusually warm and pleasant, with the stars shining brightly above. Wishing to please my boyfriend on his birthday, I let go of some of my inhibitions and we engaged in some pretty heavy necking on a secluded bench in St Stephen's park. I matured a lot that night as I discovered the pleasures of touching and being touched in intimate places. I felt desired and loved as never before, not as a daughter, sister, or friend, but as a woman.

It was a few minutes after midnight when I placed my key into the lock of the front door to our apartment. However, as I immediately discovered, there was no need for a key. My father was standing in the doorway, furious, and he swung the door open. Without a word, he lunged at me and slapped me across the face so hard that his wedding ring split my upper lip, causing extensive bleeding and pain. I had to miss three days of work before the wound closed up and the swelling subsided enough that I could show my face in public. The injury to my psyche took a lot longer to heal, and that scar has stayed forever. My parents did not talk to me for days. They called Rezsö on the carpet the very next day, however; he had to come over to our house and listen to a lecture from my father about his responsibilities as a man. He was also informed that he would not be allowed to call on me if I ever came home late again. I felt thoroughly humiliated and stayed in my room while Auntie Mariska kept me supplied with food and fresh, cold compresses to help bring down the swelling.

This incident permanently damaged my relationship with my father and took away, forever, the opportunity for a meaningful dialogue with my mother. For years, I had believed that my mother didn't understand me, so her refusal to discuss the incident with me reinforced my belief that she never would. While I am sure that both my parents felt bad about the extent of my physical injury, I don't think they realized the psychological effect this confrontation had on me and on my relationship with them. Although I still loved and respected my parents, the episode created a wall between us. They felt I owed them an apology for disobeying their rules, while I felt this had been just the latest proof of the mistreatment I had to endure, despite the fact that I had always tried my best to be a good daughter. Sadly, we never revisited the event to discuss our feelings and thus clear the air. Instead of my mother, it was my old friend, Susie, from primary school, and my new friend, Csöppi, in the attic apartment, to whom I turned with my questions and for help in sorting out my feelings.

Since Rezsö was busy with his studies during the week, for recreation after work during the week I joined a table tennis sports club. After discovering that I had some talent, I began to play competitively in singles, doubles, and mixed doubles tournaments. My consulting firm had a team competing in the city championships, and I was delighted when I earned a spot on the singles and mixed doubles roster of the company's team. Thanks to my good hand and eye coordination, combined with good ball sense, I started winning matches. Unfortunately, my hereditary condition, a slight tremor in my hands, was noticeable to the spectators and drew an occasional unkind comment, even though the trembling did not seem to impede the quality of my game.

Throughout my life, it has always been people's reaction to the tremor that is the worst part about it, for regardless of the task I am performing I have learned to compensate for the unsteadiness of my hands. However, it bothers me no end when people assume that the tremors are a manifestation of nerves and complete strangers tell me to calm down. Fortunately, my family and friends understand that this is a condition both my brother and I seem to have inherited from my father, and they are able to completely ignore the symptoms.

As the days, weeks, and months passed, my adult life was

slowly taking shape, or so I thought. I had a good profession. It was not the university graduate, scientific career I used to dream about as a young girl, but an interesting and respectable one. Slowly that old fantasy of going to college faded into the background and was hidden in a little corner of my subconscious mind, giving rise to a new dream, one I thought to be more practical, or at least more attainable. This one would include a productive career as a design draftsman, a husband with a university degree, a comfortable little apartment, and at least one child, but preferably two, a boy and a girl, or two boys.

One area where I saw a future problem was my complete lack of domestic skills. Over the years, despite my curiosity, Auntie Mariska would never allow me in the kitchen, not even to make a snack. She would take Csöppi, our young neighbor in the attic apartment, to the farmer's market and instruct her in the fine art of negotiating with the peasants for the best possible price for their produce, but not me. Never. She would teach Csöppi how to identify the freshest vegetables, the sweetest fruits, and the best cuts of meat, but not me. Never. She would share with Csöppi her art of cooking and baking, but not me. Never. No matter how I begged. She considered our kitchen to be her exclusive domain and she guarded it jealously, especially from me. I think she was afraid that if I became a good cook we might decide we had no further need for her services. I don't think she ever realized how essential and valuable she had become to our family over the years, how respected and loved she was. She was a member of the family, our surrogate grandmother.

All this changed early in the summer when Auntie Mariska slipped in the kitchen and fell, breaking her right arm. This fracture required a heavy cast with a shoulder brace to immobilize it. "Why is God punishing me in this manner?" she would ask over and over, while trying to perform her chores with her left hand. I think she regarded the considerable physical discomfort as minor when compared to the emotional distress she had to endure due to her inability to use her right arm. My brother and I both helped with the cleaning and the dishes. For eight weeks, she had to have me around as she ran the household and she had to take me along with her to the market, a task we did on Saturday afternoons. "At least we can get some bargains," she consoled herself in a low voice while complaining loudly to the peasants about the quality of their produce left over from the morning. She had to do her cooking and baking verbally, while I followed her instructions, though never to her satisfaction. "Faster," she would urge me, "at this rate, the carrots will never be scraped clean, and look at those potatoes. You are peeling them too thick. You are wasting your parents' hard-earned money. We have no pigs to which we could feed the scraps." And so it went every day after I got home from work. If I hadn't felt sorry for her, I would have laughed out loud at times, but I restrained myself, even after she told me that I was "hopeless." It must have been pure hell for the poor old woman, while I had delight in my good fortune acquiring the fundamentals of home-making from the very best model. I hated housecleaning with a passion, but I enjoyed cooking and baking, as well as the tasty meals I managed to produce. Not only did I learn the arts of cooking and baking, but I also learned to love and respect the culinary arts, for which I remain forever grateful to Auntie Mariska.

I was acutely aware that the biggest obstacle to my new dreams of a home of my own was the lack of available apartments in Budapest. Many young couples had to move in with one or the other set of parents when they got married, hoping that sooner or later an apartment would turn up. Nothing ever did, unless a member of the family had connections in the government or was a good communist. Rezső's older brother moved into a small room in his parents' apartment with his new wife and baby and stayed there for years until he found a job and an apartment in a provincial city. Assuming that my relationship was to mature into a serious commitment with Rezsö, the only place left for us would have been my parents' home, and I was determined not to live there, even if I never got married.

Then to my great joy, one day I discovered that there was a way out, even if it was five, or six years down the road. A few young designers from my consulting engineering firm (including me) established a partnership with a few young tradesmen from a construction company. We scoured the city for suitable attic or basement areas that could be converted into small apartments. One of us would expropriate the space through the housing agency, and then we would obtain the necessary permits, prepare a design according to the building codes, and assist the tradesmen with the construction. We also contributed a nominal amount of money each month for materials. Everybody worked for free, donating their time and specific expertise, for the chance of eventually getting one of these apartments when their turn came. I was delighted when I was conditionally accepted into the group, provided I had a fiancé's name to submit. While I was in no hurry to get married and claim an apartment, I was assured of being able to obtain one in due time.

Rezsö was still studying at the university and had neither income nor a steady job. I didn't know how to approach him about submitting his name along with mine to the cooperative for an apartment, until one day he told me how difficult it was for his brother, Gyuri, to be living in one room with his family at their apartment. "I would never get married, if that was the only solution," he informed me, "so I guess I'll just have to stay a bachelor." That was my opening, and I went for it. "There is another possible way out," I said, "although you would have to ask me to marry you." I explained the situation. "Nobody from our families has to know about it," I assured him, "and the document we sign proclaiming our engagement is not legally binding." By mutual agreement, when I completed the paperwork, next to my name as the major applicant, his was placed in the fiancé column. I wasn't sure if that meant that we were engaged or not, but I was excited and happy. I was young, I had possibilities for a better life, with time to plan and build. I had Something to Love, Something to Do, and Something to Hope for.

Chapter Seven

THE REVOLUTION

B ecause Stalin had no designated successor, after his death in 1953 there followed a series of lesser political personalities in the leadership position of the Soviet Union. In February 1956, a relatively unknown man named Nikita Khrushchev was rumored to have delivered a so-called secret speech at a Soviet Communist Party Congress, denouncing the extreme policies and practices of the Stalin years. This event is now considered to be the beginning of the de-Stalinization of the Soviet Union and its satellite countries. Khrushchev managed to grab and consolidate power in the party apparatus and later in the government, and he maintained his leadership until he was deposed in 1964.

During the summer of 1956, there were rumors circulating in Budapest of anti-government riots in East Germany that had been quickly put down by the army. At the same time, we heard that there was also Polish defiance against the Soviet rule, which culminated in the unsuccessful Poznan uprising. Limited as the defiance in Poland was, however, it represented a small crack in the communists' perceived armor of invincibility.

Meanwhile, Tito, the renegade Yugoslav communist leader, was quietly fanning the flames of discontent all over Eastern Europe, particularly in Hungary.

It didn't take much to awaken the Hungarians' sense of indignation against the injustices of the past, for these fiercely independent people were already close to the boiling point. Living standards were abominable. Personal and political freedom were nonexistent. To ease the situation, Khrushchev had Mátyás Rákosi replaced as party secretary by Ernö Gerö, a lesser known communist who was equally loyal to Moscow, and by Imre Nagy as prime minister. Nagy was later replaced by one of Gerö's more trusted allies, András Hegedüs. Injustices of the past were blamed on Rákosi and former Soviet Secret Service chief Lavrenti Beria, who was later executed in Moscow for crimes committed under Stalin. During the period leading up to 1956, many political prisoners in Hungary were released and rehabilitated, some posthumously, like László Rajk, whose only crime had been to sympathize with Tito's brand of communism.

Slowly, the political climate seemed to become less repressive. Newspaper articles became more open and radio commentaries less one-sided. Discussion groups, labeled "literary circles," sprang up all over the city, the most prominent being the Petöfi Circle, named after Sándor Petöfi, a young romantic poet and hero of the 1848 revolution against the Hapsburg Empire, who had died on the battlefield at age twenty-six. The irony of the situation lay in the fact that these groups originated in the DISZ association headquarters and were organized by young, idealistic, communist intellectuals.

I never attended any of the discussion groups. I wasn't very literary, and, besides, my parents would have been mortified to find me participating, fearing the possible negative consequences of dissent on my career. "Don't expose yourself to danger. Keep your thoughts to yourself," my father would counsel us constantly. So I just kept myself informed by listening to accounts of the literary circles' activities from friends. Then, in late October, there were rumors of a march being organized by the Writers' and Artists' Union and university students to show solidarity with Polish workers demonstrating for more freedom and against economic hardship.

On October 23, 1956, when I left home for work on that cold, foggy Tuesday morning, I had no notion of the momentous events that were going to unfold that day. As I stepped out of the building, a chilly gust of wind blowing from the river hit me, taking my breath away, and I was glad I had decided to wear my winter coat. But except for the gloomy weather, nothing looked out of the ordinary as I struggled against the wind on my way to the streetcar terminus at the foot of Margaret Bridge.

As usual, I was on the Pest side of the river, traveling on the Number Two tram as it was winding its way on its tracks, which hugged the east bank of the Danube and briefly left the river to curve around Kossuth Square in front of the magnificent Parliament Building. On the surface, things appeared ordinary, but gradually I became aware of an unmistakable sense of excitement in the air.

People around me were talking about a student convention being held that morning at the Technical University. Somebody mentioned that a procession was being planned for two o'clock in the afternoon to march to the statue of the Polish general, Joseph Bem, who in the 1848 Revolution had come to fight on the side of the Hungarians against the Hapsburg rule. The people around me on the tram seemed to be throwing caution to the wind. They were openly exchanging information about the anticipated events of that afternoon with complete strangers, apparently without any fear. I listened with amazement and began to share their sense of excitement.

I spent the whole morning in the office, working at my desk and seemingly oblivious to the world around me. But my mind was on developments about to unfold on the streets outside. At that time, Rezsö was attending his last semester at the Technical University. Were he and his friends, Iván and Robie, going to be among the student marchers? I didn't know, although my guess was that they probably were. I was sure that Johnny and his friends, Laci and Gömbi, were going to participate. What will my best friend, Lia, do, I wondered, or Susie, or some of my former classmates? What about Csöppi? Because she worked as a manicurist in a downtown establishment frequented by party insiders and their spouses, she always knew every rumor that circulated in Budapest. Would she join in the march? But none of us knew anything about the students' preparations, so we had made no arrangements to meet. Should I try to get in touch with somebody? Why isn't someone calling me? I wondered, although I knew full well that telephones were at a premium and lines were always busy. One did not call people at their workplace unless it was an emergency, so I didn't even try.

At lunchtime, I decided to walk the three blocks from the office to the Danube River. I wanted to see for myself what was happening. The demonstrators heading to the statue of General Bem from the university on either side of the riverbank had to pass by where I would be standing. I was astonished at what I saw that day.

As the Danube was steadily flowing downstream, exactly as it had done for centuries, on both of its banks throngs of people were walking just as steadily upstream, heading toward Bem Square. "These are not university students," I thought to myself. Immediately, I realized that these were people who had left their jobs in offices and factories, people like me, who wanted to know, who wanted to be seen and heard, who wanted to lend their support to the students' voices.

I decided to make my way to a monument erected to the poet Sándor Petöfi which was located just a couple of blocks away. Something was sure to happen there, I thought, and I was right. The large square was filling up rapidly in anticipation of the rumored arrival of members of the Petöfi Literary Circle who, it was assumed, planned to read a sixteen-point ultimatum they had formulated at the student meeting that morning.

I was fortunate to find a spot on the steps of the monument, to the left and in front of the statue, where I could hear and see what was happening. People were talking openly and exchanging ideas. A young actor named Imre Sinkovich appeared at the foot of the statue holding a volume of Petöfi's works. He started to recite a patriotic poem by Petöfi titled "Song of Our Nation" (*Nemzeti Dal*) that was a call to arms during the 1848 revolution and was likely to stir just as strong nationalistic sentiments a century later.

Arise Magyars. Your Homeland is calling.
The time is now. Now, or never.
We can be slaves, or we can be free.
That is the question. Make your choices.

The crowd listened, then joined in, repeating the ancient, well-known refrain after each stanza: "*We swear by the God of the Magyars that we won't be slaves any more!*" Each person raised their right arm, hand in a fist with the index and middle finger extended pointing to the sky, just as their ancestors had done little over a century earlier. I looked up and noticed that the statue's right arm was raised in exactly the same gesture.

Next, a young tenor stepped up and started to sing another well-known patriotic piece, "Manifesto" (*Szózat*), by the poet, Kölcsey Ferenc, to the lovely melody of the composer, Erkel Ferenc. "*To your homeland, steadfastly, be faithful, oh Magyar ...,*" we all listened silently, the words and the music resonating in our hearts.

Finally everybody joined in singing the Hungarian national anthem, "*God bless the Magyars...*" Tears were streaming down my face as I sang along at the top of my voice. Something significant was happening, and I was a participant as well as a witness to these events.

Meanwhile, multitudes of people kept streaming by, heading for Bem Square. From my vantage point, I had a great view beyond the square and toward the banks of the Danube. I noticed that many of the marchers were carrying the tricolor (red, white, and green) flag of Hungary. I had to look again, as in the gentle breeze I saw more and more flags with a circular hole in the middle in place of the communist crest. A bystander informed me that one of the students' demands was the reinstatement of the old historic crest of Hungary instead of the Soviet style crest the communists had imposed after they seized power in 1949.

I looked at my watch and noted that my lunch period was long over. I should be back at my desk. "Too late," I thought, "I don't care." The streets were filled with people walking shoulder to shoulder, as far as the eye could see, on both sides of the Danube and on the bridges spanning the river. It was an incredible sight. Suddenly I caught a glimpse of my brother, Johnny, on the other side of the square sitting on the shoulders of his two friends. I was not alone.

When the members of the Petöfi Literary Circle arrived to read the sixteen-point manifesto, we were ready to hear it and roared our approval after each point. The profound demands cut across the political and economic fabric of the country, starting with the immediate withdrawal of the Soviet troops from Hungary. But how realistic was that? How could we hope to win? I didn't know, and at that instant it didn't seem to matter. I just knew that we believed in our cause being just and wanted to add our voices to the protest movement. We knew of no plan, we had no instructions from a central authority. Without regard to common sense, each of us proceeded in our own self-appointed task born of the moment.

The young men of the Petöfi Circle announced that they were going to present their document to legislators in the Parliament House on Kossuth Square. I followed them to the square, which was on my way home, anyway. It was getting late, so there was no point going back to the office. Although I kept an eye out for friends, there were thousands of people in the square, in the side streets, and it seemed utterly hopeless to find anybody I knew. The buses and streetcars had stopped running, as people spilled over from the sidewalks to the road and on to the tracks, blocking the trams' path.

As I was making my way across the square, I was becoming increasingly frightened at the rapid turn of events. Earlier, at the insistence of the crowd gathered in front of the Parliament, Imre Nagy had appeared on a balcony of the interior ministry building across the street and started to speak, but few could hear him. He seemed to me to be a small figure swept up by big events, unable to have any effect on them.

Rumors were rampant. "The students are heading for the main radio station to have their manifesto read over the airwaves," said one young man. "Factory workers from Csepel are going to use blowtorches on Hero's Square, near the eastern railway station, to cut down the giant bronze statue of Stalin," said another, starting out in that direction with a couple of his friends. I would have loved to see that, and I was tempted to join them, but it was too far for me to walk and I was tired. People were chanting slogans like "Russians go home," and "we want free elections." With time, more and more red, white, and green Hungarian flags appeared in windows, some adorned with the old traditional crest. On one street corner, an old lady was handing out small red, white, and green ribbons with pins for boutonnieres. Everybody seemed to be acting on impulse, doing what they could to relieve the pressure built up by years of repression and frustration. "Where will it all lead?" I wondered. At the same time that I had a sense of uneasiness, I also felt a sense of excitement and elation as events were unfolding.

As dusk was settling over the square, I realized that except for a light breakfast, I had had nothing to eat the whole day. After all the excitement, shouting, and singing, I began to feel cold, as well as tired, hungry, lonely, and scared, so I decided to call it a day and head home through the crowded streets.

It was dark, well after nine o'clock, when I finally got home, to the great relief of my parents. Trying to be objective, I gave them a short account of my experiences. There was no sign of my brother, and although I was worried, I thought it wise not to tell them that I had seen him earlier with his friends at the demonstration. I tried to call Rezsö from the corner telephone booth, but could not get a line, so eventually I gave up, not knowing where he was and what he was doing. (Because of his father's job at the news agency, his family was one of the few private citizens who did have a telephone at home.)

My parents and Auntie Mariska were outright frantic about Johnny's whereabouts. If I knew my brother and his friends, they were in the thick of things and I could tell that that was on the minds of my parents, too, and causing them extreme anxiety. He never did come home that night, and he never did tell us exactly what he and the others had been doing.

I got up very early the next morning to find my parents, who probably had never gone to bed, glued to the radio. My brother was nowhere. The announcer on the radio was parroting the official party line about the counterrevolutionaries who were trying to create unrest. We knew how to listen between the lines, but it still did not make the situation on the streets clear to us. We realized that there had been some sort of an armed confrontation at the radio station during the night and that there were casualties. However, according to the announcer, because of the quick "heroic" action of the security forces, normalcy had been restored and people were urged to go about their regular daily business.

From my experiences the day before, I knew that there was no way things on the streets were back to normal, as the radio announcer claimed. The crowds I had seen the day before downtown and in front of the Parliament House on Kossuth Square would not all have gone home peacefully without some resolution to their cause. Regardless of my arguments to the contrary, my father was adamant that I go to work, and my mother concurred. My parents were worried, that if I didn't show up at the office that morning, people were going to think that I was participating in the "counterrevolutionary" activities. "You could lose your job, or worse yet, be investigated, charged, jailed, or deported," my father warned me. Against my better judgment, I set off to go to work around eight o'clock that morning.

As soon as I got near the tram stop at the foot of Margaret Bridge, I realized that I was right. Things were far from normal. To my amazement, on the major ring road leading to the tram terminal, I saw men with rifles on their shoulders heading in the opposite direction from the bridge, toward the Western Railroad Station. There were army trucks heading in the same direction as well. Never since the war had I seen a civilian carrying a rifle. It was against the law for citizens to own firearms.

Reaching the stop, I discovered that the streetcars were not running. Oh well, I thought, I will just have to walk, and I started out on the forty-five minute walk to the office, not thinking that I would have to cross Kossuth Square in front of the Parliament House on my way. Under the current circumstances, that route could be dangerous. I was also unaware of the fact that, about twenty minutes after I left home, a curfew was announced over the radio till one o'clock in the afternoon. My parents must have been worried sick, as they had sent me out into the streets just minutes earlier.

I emerged from a small side street to the sight of Russian tanks in front of the Parliament Building. There was not a living soul in sight and nothing moved in the eerie silence that seemed to envelop the square. I wasn't thinking straight, for I continued walking on the sidewalk next to the ministry buildings on the opposite side, parallel to the Parliament. I didn't notice the lifeless bodies lying on the ground around the tanks. When I finally did notice them, I just stared in disbelief. The dead wore no military uniforms. They were clearly civilians. Some were young, some old, men, women and even children, and none had guns. As I lifted my eyes from this almost unbearable sight, I saw the AVO secret service machine gun positions on the roofs of the ministry buildings surrounding three sides of the square. It was members of the dreaded AVO secret service who had shot those demonstrators, not the Russian tanks. What evil could have made them shoot their own people?

When a volley of shots rang out, the reality of my situation penetrated my consciousness and the flight instinct took over. I turned on my heels and ran back as fast as I could, while bullets ricocheted off the building behind me. Finally, shaking like a leaf, I ducked into the closest side street. Did I have a guardian angel protecting me from harm that morning, deflecting those bullets? Or was it possible that those soldiers missed on purpose? The Russian soldiers had strict orders to shoot to kill all of us "fascist provocateurs and bourgeois revolutionaries." However, they had been stationed in Hungary long enough to recognize the truth, that in reality they were facing innocent, ordinary citizens, the kind they themselves were in civilian life back home.

One would think I had had enough warning by then. I should have turned around to go home, but for some reason, perhaps curiosity, I didn't turn. Instead, I took a big detour and finally made it to the office. Hardly anybody was there. I signed in, but I did not feel like working. I kept trying to telephone Rezsö, but the telephone lines were overloaded and I never reached him. I had no idea what he and his friends were doing and I was worried about them.

Some of the other employees and I sat around in the office talking, listening to the radio. It was announced that Imre Nagy was appointed again as prime minister. He immediately appealed to the fighters to stop and lay down their arms. Deadlines were announced, then moved several times until they were finally abandoned. It became known that armed rebels had taken over major factories, establishing workers' councils, not only in Budapest, but in other major cities as well. They were not going to just give up, not without concessions from the government.

One of the engineers had a short-wave radio, and a group

was trying to listen through the crackling of the jamming stations to the Voice of America, Radio Free Europe, and the BBC. A couple went to the bus depot near Deák Square and returned with the latest information from bus drivers and taxi drivers. The few telephones were busy all the time now, with friends asking for and providing news from all over the city.

There was another reason why people did not heed Nagy's urgings to stop protesting and return to work. The despised Gerö remained party secretary, and everybody knew that that was the position where the real power originated. People also heard and believed the rumors that Gerö was the one who had ordered the secret police to shoot at demonstrators the night before in front of the radio building and the Parliament House. Worst of all, he was the one who had invited the Soviet troops to take up positions in strategic locations in Budapest, providing them with the pretext to intervene. The sentiment on the street was that Gerö had to go.

By afternoon, the situation all around the city had deteriorated, and armed men and the dreaded AVO secret police were hunting each other. The night before, Pál Maléter, a young communist colonel, had rallied a handful of his soldiers and taken over the Kilián Army Barracks, close to downtown Pest, and successfully defended it from Russian tanks. The barracks became the source of guns and ammunition for throngs of young people who acquired firearms and turned into freedom fighters. The curfew announced that morning expired by early afternoon. According to rumor, the streets were getting truly dangerous, especially around the routes I needed to take home.

One of my colleagues lived on the Buda side, near where Rezsö lived, so I decided that instead of heading home alone, I was going to go with him and find out what Rezsö and his friends were doing. "Once I am there, I can always double back on the west side of the Danube and cross back to Pest on Margaret Bridge to go home," I rationalized to myself.

Rezsö's whole family was home when I arrived on their doorstep. To say that they were astonished at the sight of me as Rezsö opened the door would be an understatement. Rezsö seemed embarrassed and told me off in no uncertain terms for my foolishness in wandering the streets. To his rational engineer's mind, I had made a succession of errors in judgment. Although he must have been flattered by the fact that I cared to go to great lengths to find him, I could tell that he was annoyed. I tried to explain my presence, minimizing the effort, and assured them that I intended to head home right away. Of course, Rezsö's parents would not let me leave, especially not alone, and neither would they risk letting their son accompany me on what they considered to be an extremely dangerous journey.

I had to telephone a neighbor in our apartment house, who went to get my father. The poor man had no choice, but to accept Elsa Mama's assurances that I was going to be completely safe in their home and give his permission for me to stay. His darling daughter sleeping in her boyfriend's home — that must have been a bitter pill for this straight-laced man to swallow. However, by sending me to work earlier that morning, he had put me in the path of danger with nearly fatal consequences. He didn't dare do it again, so he felt he had no choice but to agree to my staying there. I was told that my brother had not come home yet, either. I felt truly sorry for my father and wished I had tried to return home from work instead of going to check on Rezsö, but I could not undo what was already done.

Next morning, as several Russian tanks rumbled past the square, one stopped beneath the second floor balcony of the apartment. I foolishly peered out the window for a better look. One of the tank's crew must have seen me, for to my horror, I saw the turret on top of the tank beginning to turn ever so slowly in my direction. Oh, God — one bullet from that big gun, and the whole side of the building will be gone, with me in it. The thought came to me in a flash, and I wet my pants from fright. I was completely frozen on the spot. *Rat-a-tat-tat-tat*, I heard the by-then familiar sounds of a volley of shots from a machine gun, leaving its trace of holes to this day above the balcony door. Crouching motionless under the window and watching the tank leave, all I could think of was that if they had used their big gun, there would be a big gaping hole where I was kneeling and I would be dead for sure. For some reason, God had spared me again.

Robie Bán, one of Rezsö's best friends, stopped by the second evening of my stay, and we talked for a long time. He was very optimistic about our future in a free Hungary. His vision was that Hungary would be a neutral country like Austria and Switzerland, protected and supported by the powerful nations of the west. He explained his vision enthusiastically. I liked Robie a lot, and I remember hugging and kissing him good-bye as he left. That was the last time I saw him alive.

Three days passed, before I was allowed to go home. I took the Number Eighteen streetcar, on the Buda side of the Danube, admiring the beautiful, gothic Parliament Building and its reflection in the river as we passed by. I wasn't going to risk passing in front of Parliament House and Kossuth Square on the Pest side again, although according to rumors, the Russian tanks were gone, replaced by friendly Hungarian guards who were Pál Maléter's men. Ernö Gerö had been relieved of his post and had been replaced by János Kádár as First Secretary of the Communist Party, forming yet another new government.

We constantly listened to the radio for news. We kept switching stations from Radio Kossuth, and Radio Petöfi (both government stations in Budapest) and to Radio Free Europe, the Voice of America, or the BBC on short wave. Before October 23, the communists had been constantly jamming the western radio stations making it almost impossible to listen to them, but now all of these stations could be heard loud and clear. The novelty of hearing differing points of views on the same subject was invigorating.

All the while, my father was certain that it was just a matter of days before the Russians were going to reestablish a communist regime by force and that the West would stand by without interfering. My mother was hopeful, but I thought the communists were finished in Hungary. They had lost the support of the very people they proclaimed to represent: the young intellectuals, the workers, and the farmers. Meanwhile, my brother was God-knows-where, already building the new Hungary. Johnny and I were idealistic, my father realistic. However, Auntie Mariska knew best; she went to the farmers market to stock up on food.

It was not a complete surprise when, in the early morning hours of November 4, Imre Nagy announced a Soviet attack on Budapest. Earlier, unbeknownst to him, members of the revolutionary government, including Pál Maléter, had been lured into a "safe-conduct" meeting where the Russians placed them under arrest. Backed by Soviet troops, a new communist government had been formed with János Kádár, a traitor to his comrades and the revolution, as prime minister. Imre Nagy took refuge in the Yugoslav embassy, but a few days later he and his aides were tricked into leaving the grounds right into the arms of the KGB, the Russian secret police. They were promptly imprisoned and executed in 1958.

There was fighting all over the city and in the countryside, but, unless the NATO countries were going to act quickly to stop the Soviet invasion, the outcome was never in doubt. NATO didn't come, and the Russians, having counted on the inaction of the west, proceeded ruthlessly to reestablish their dominance over the freedom-loving people of Hungary.

Within days in a small nation of ten million people, thousands died on the streets and in prisons, while many more thousands were rounded up and carted off to Siberia, never to be seen again. The overall losses were estimated to be close to three hundred thousand. But there were also lucky ones, two hundred thousand strong, who managed to cross the border to the west and start a new life of freedom and opportunity.

The Kilián Army barracks after the November 4, 1956
invasion by the Russians

Budapest after the crushing of the 1956 revolution

The aftermath of the 1956 Russian invasion

Chapter Eight

BREAKING FREE

During the spring and summer, only a short time before the 1956 revolution that started on October 23, as part of Khrushchev's "de-Stalinization" policies, the Hungarian army had removed the iron curtain, that is, the barbed wire fence with its minefields, on the Austro-Hungarian border. Thus, fortuitously, for a short while there was a relatively safe escape route open to those who felt they needed to leave Hungary after the Russian troops crushed the uprising.

Following the Russian invasion on November 4, and drawing the inevitable and very painful conclusion that the revolution was over, people took widely diverging paths. Sadly, Russian and AVO bullets took care of some with deadly finality. Others knew instantly that they needed to run for their lives, and they left their homeland without delay. Many more hesitated, uncertain about the direction to take, and some postponed the decision until it became progressively more dangerous, and eventually impossible, to leave Hungary. This small nation of ten million people lost about five hundred thousand of its citizens during the revolution and its aftermath.

Following the influx of fresh Russian troops, fighting continued and pockets of resistance were slowly and brutally eliminated by the end of the year, leaving the city in ruins. Some said it was worse than after the Second World War. Initially, the freedom fighters believed that the United States and her allies in

NATO would come to the aid of the revolution, but with time it became evident that the West had abandoned us. The fresh troops the Russians mobilized to subdue Budapest were from Mongolia, reportedly two hundred thousand strong, with twenty-five hundred tanks. The communists didn't trust their regular troops to shoot Hungarians, cruelly put down the resistance in the capital, and subjugate the citizens in the smaller cities and the countryside.

About a week after the invasion, the streetcars and buses started running again and people were ordered back to work, although the universities remained closed.

My brother was seldom home during this period. He would appear, mostly to eat, get cleaned up and grab a few winks, before disappearing again. This continued until just past the middle of November, when one evening at dinner, he calmly informed my parents that the next morning he and two of his friends, Laci and Gömbi, would be heading for the Austrian border.

My father was obviously torn. He did not know what to say, and his pain was clearly visible. Deep down he knew my brother had made the right decision, yet he didn't want to part with his only son. The fact that Johnny had walked in one day with a gun helped soften his opposition. After all, he reasoned, "If anybody has seen you and reports you, they are going to hang you anyway, so you might as well make a run for it."

It was much worse though for my poor mother, who became hysterical. "I won't let you go. I'll lie down across the threshold to stop you," she threatened, tears running down her cheeks. "Then I'll just step over you," my brother replied firmly, putting his arms around her shoulders and trying to soften the blow. "You don't understand. I have to go," he continued in a more conciliatory tone, wiping away her tears.

Auntie Mariska was softly crying in the kitchen. I begged Johnny to take me along, but he refused, saying he did not want the responsibility. "If we get caught, you don't want to be arrested in my company," was his cryptic explanation. "Look on the bright side," he continued. "You will have our room all to yourself." However, my father quickly put an end to the discussion. "Forget it," was his curt but firm advice to me, cutting short my protestations.

Next morning we all got up at four A.M. for my brother's last breakfast at home: chocolate milk, Hungarian *téli* salami sandwiches, and fresh pancakes. Auntie Mariska informed us that we had nothing to worry about, because she had prayed to Saint Anthony and offered him a two hundred *forint* donation for helping her beloved *Janika* safely across the border. She assured us that he would be safe and everything was going to be just fine. Then it was time to say good-bye, each of us trying to hide our pain for the sake of the others.

Later that morning, my father and I went to work, but my mother had to call in sick. She stayed in bed, crying, the whole day under the care of Auntie Mariska. She was in double torment, worried about my brother's safety and, at the same time, mourning his departure. She knew the high probability that she would never be able to see him again.

We were constantly listening to the Voice of America hoping to hear my brother's coded message, signaling that he had made it safely across the border. Understanding messages through the incessant crackling of the airwaves had become difficult again, for the communists were again continuously jamming broadcasts from the west. In addition, the communications being sent by the refugees were coded, because people did not want to give their real names for fear of reprisals later against the relatives who were left behind.

The list of messages would go on and on. We could not believe the numbers. Finally, after about a week, we heard the anticipated words, "The blue eagle and his two companions have landed." After we heard the message repeated and we were convinced we heard it right, we were finally able to rejoice in Johnny's success. We had kept his departure a secret from others. I noticed though, that Pityu, the young university professor across the corridor from us was not around any more, nor was Marika, the ballerina from the apartment across from ours on the fourth floor, and Aunt Mici's son, Joseph, the famous scientist, was nowhere to be seen either. Of course, Auntie Mariska knew where everybody was. She hadn't lived in this building for close to twenty years not to know everybody's business. She told me in confidence that all these people and some others, as well, had left for the west.

I dutifully went to work every day, feeling thoroughly depressed about the future of the country in general and myself in particular. Stories abounded about the reprisals and brutality of the Russians and the AVO secret service men. At the office, there was a rumor circulating that we all were going to be interviewed individually by the company's security officer about our whereabouts and activities during what the freshly reintroduced, prevailing communist propaganda labeled to be the "counterrevolutionary" period.

I started wrestling with the idea of leaving the country myself, and eventually became obsessed with it. I could not help thinking how fortunate my brother was in having made it to freedom safely, as opposed to me, still stuck in communist Hungary. I was not looking forward to having to go back to living the lies, deceits, and duplicities of the past. On the other hand, I felt guilty about leaving my parents, especially my mother with her poor health. Would she survive losing both of her children, or would this be the final blow that broke her heart? However, the thought of becoming independent of the strict, much-resented parental control and free of the oppressive environment of the communist regime appealed to me greatly. As I had done so often in the past, I went to the Franciscan church, sat in Franz Liszt's seat for a long time, listened to the organ music, and discussed my predicament with God.

Next morning, I called Rezsö and asked him to meet me for lunch near my office. The university was still closed, so he was free. The restaurant was filled with the usual lunchtime crowd. "I don't want to live in a communist Hungary," I informed him in a hushed tone, "I am getting out. I am leaving tomorrow morning, with or without you." He was not at all surprised to hear what I had to say. He had been expecting it for days, he told me, and he had been thinking about the move himself, discussing it with his father at length. "It will be *with* me tomorrow," he responded without the slightest hesitation, "and with me for the rest of our lives as well, if you marry me," he added, reaching for my hand. After some discussion, we agreed to meet the following morning at six at the southern railway station in Buda, to take a train to a border town, where we would try and cross into Austria together. We sealed our pact with a kiss.

Already it was the last day of November, and the cold winter weather was setting in, and the days were getting shorter, the nights longer. Crossing the border was becoming more dangerous, as the communists consolidated their power. They were plugging the holes in the Hungarian border defenses with freshly deployed Russian-armed troops from Mongolia. We knew we had no time to waste.

Heartbroken as my parents were on hearing my decision, they did not try to dissuade me. Had they allowed me to go with my brother, I would have been safe already. They could not escape that guilt. "Dangerous as it is to try to escape this late," I argued, "staying could be just as bad, if not worse." I assured them that Rezsö and I intended to get married as soon as possible and that I would not do anything impulsive, unless I discussed it in my mind with them and obtained their approval.

Ever practical, Auntie Mariska appeared with the building superintendent's two sons, Feri, aged twenty, and Pista, fifteen, both students. They announced with a wink, that they were going to the border town of Sopron for a visit with their aunt who lived there and asked if I would I like to join them, perhaps with a friend. It was agreed that we were going to visit their aunt the next day, Friday. My father was going to call my office and report me sick in bed with a temperature.

After dinner, I found time to visit Csöppi, and her family in their small upstairs attic apartment to say good-bye. My usually cheerful friend, this time without her ever-present smile, did her best to try to dissuade me from leaving. "You have a good job, family, friends who love you," she said. "Don't risk your life trying to leave," she pled, tears in her eyes. Little Zsuzsi cuddled quietly in my lap, her head against my breast, her doll in her arms. I hugged and kissed them as I hurried out the door. It was hard to depart, but my mind was made up.

Later, lying in my bed, I thought of all the things I had said that I should not have said, all the places I had been where I should not have been, and the things I had done that I should not have done during the few days when we thought we were free. I was convinced that those things added to my already tarnished image with the communists and would most certainly put my future in Hungary in jeopardy. All it would take was for a jealous coworker to report on me and I could lose my job, be deported, taken to Siberia, or confined to a correctional institution. As far as I knew, I did not have a single enemy who would do that to me, yet I was well aware of the thousands of innocent people who had been betrayed during the communists' rule in just such a manner. People would disappear during the night for no apparent reason, never to be seen again. No trials, no due process, no appeals. Those things happened all the time.

When all was quiet, I got up and went through my secret memory box, which was hidden under my bed. I reread Peter's love letters one by one, then tossed them into the fire in the big glazed-tile, wood-burning stove that stood in the corner of the room my brother and I had shared but which for the past two weeks had been mine alone. The familiar voice in the little corner of my heart asked if I was making the biggest mistake of my life by not contacting Peter before leaving, but my mind reassured me that I was following my destiny. After all, if he still cared, he could have, *he should have*, contacted me. Still, I could not help wondering though if I'd ever see Peter again. I kissed his picture good-bye before tossing it into the flames and watching it turn to ashes. Then I closed the little cast iron door on the stove, leaving the ashes and my first love behind. (However, I found out with time that his image, always tucked away in the little corner of my heart, could not be as easily obliterated.)

Finally, I put my secret bankbook on my bedroom table in an envelope with my mother's name on it, enclosing deposits of the equivalent of about six months' salary. I wrote instructions for my parents to spend the money to take a taxi to the fancy restaurant at the Grand Hotel on Margaret Island at Christmas to rejoice in their children's bright future. Having put my affairs in order, I finally fell asleep, at peace with my decision to leave.

Next morning, for the second time in two weeks, we all got up at four A.M. again, but this time it was for my last breakfast at home. I had asked for chocolate milk, buttered toast with sardines, and fresh pancakes. After a restful night, I woke up to the voice of Auntie Mariska saying, "Rise and shine," accompanied by a gentle kiss on my forehead. With tears in her eyes, she immediately retreated to the kitchen. I quickly washed up in the bathroom and got dressed in the layers of clothing the family council had laid out for me the night before against the cold weather. My one and only bra which I seldom wore (in accordance with the European custom of the times), and panties first, then nylon stockings, long-johns with matching long sleeved wool camisole, long wool pants and a wool sweater, and, topping it all, a gray wool pleated skirt and a white cotton blouse. Two pairs of wool socks inside my leather boots gave me difficulty in lacing them up until my father helped. My mother made herself busy checking my small backpack, making sure all essentials were there: toothbrush, toothpaste, a small soap, facecloth, cotton handkerchiefs, thermos with hot coffee, sandwiches, cookies, valuables, and money. It was still pitch dark outside. I wasn't worried about the journey that lay ahead, just incredibly excited. I never seriously considered the danger I was heading into. The possibility of not making it to Austria and beyond did not trouble me. God had protected me through many turbulent times before, I reassured myself; He would not abandon me now. With the arrogance (or is it ignorance?) of youth, I was confident in the successful conclusion of my journey.

During breakfast, Auntie Mariska had uncharacteristically disappeared from the kitchen. Her eyes were red when she returned a few minutes later, sobbing. "Don't think I loved you any less than I did your brother. I loved you both the same," she announced as she placed the fresh pancakes in front of me. Then she hugged and kissed me as she continued resolutely, "I am going to give money to Saint Anthony for you, too, when he guides you safely across the border." I was touched and asked her jokingly "Really? You are going to give him two hundred *forints* for me, too, as you did for my brother?" Her reply came without hesitation, "Nooooo, only a hundred." This broke the ice. Even my poor mother burst out laughing.

I was getting impatient to leave, as I was getting too hot under the layers of warm clothes I had piled on myself against the cold weather. My father helped me with my thick wool winter coat, which felt very tight. A pair of wool gloves and another pair of wool mittens on top of them, and a long scarf on my head completed my traveling outfit. I managed to steal a last glance at the tubby young girl in the hall mirror before hugging and kissing everybody good-bye.

I heard the front door of our apartment close behind me as I headed for the swinging doors leading to the stairwell. I did not look back. As I was descending the stairs, I counted them one last time, just as I had as a little girl, wondering if I would ever get to do this again. Hopefully, there would be other stairs, in other buildings, I thought. One day, I might even be able to return with my children and count these stairs again, I assured myself, just before spotting Feri and Pista in the downstairs hallway, waiting for me.

The two boys and I met up with Rezsö at the railway station. I spotted his familiar tall figure in the crowded station right away, dressed in his dark gray topcoat and dark gray hat over his best light gray suit. I thought he looked funny with his black earmuffs under the narrow brimmed fedora, while he teased me about the long wool scarf covering my head. He was alone, as his best friend, Iván Sós, had apparently left already for Austria, and Robie Bán, his other friend, was also missing. "How typical of Iván to leave without letting us know," I said. "All he ever thinks of is himself. Robie is a different matter though, I am worried about him." Ever practical, Rezsö responded with a stern, "Forget them, we need to focus on ourselves now," as we headed for the ticket counter.

We had to stand in a long line in front of a small window to buy our tickets. The place was crowded, and everybody seemed to be heading in the same general direction—west. Our little group decided to take a less traveled route toward our destination, the border town of Sopron, than other people seemed to be taking.

Apparently we chose a good time of the day for our departure. It was a little past six in the morning, still dark. The soldiers on night patrol were cold and sleepy and were having their morning coffee somewhere, while the rest of the secret police were probably still turning over in their bunk beds back in the barracks. There wasn't a single uniform in sight. I took a deep breath. So far, so good, I told myself.

We found seats near the front of the train, and as soon as the locomotive started to pull out of the station, I felt myself relax.

As I glanced ahead at a bend in the tracks, I got a glimpse of the majestic, black steam engine with its shiny wheels up front. It looked just like the ones I used to admire as a little girl during visits with Auntie Mariska to the western railway station. This time, though, I wasn't just watching the smoke disappear in the distance while standing on the platform. This time I was seated in a first-class compartment behind the smokestack, headed for a distant land, just as I had imagined I would be one day. The first hurdles had been taken. We had our tickets. We had not been arrested in Budapest as we boarded the train, and nobody had taken away our personal identity cards either.

A young couple with three children asked to join the four of us in our small cubicle, which was designed for six adults. We were cramped, but we did not have the heart to refuse, as the couple looked tired and dejected. They had been up all night, they told us, preparing for the journey ahead. Just the same, they looked well groomed and the children were obviously well cared for. The youngest child, a boy, was about six months old, the middle one, also a boy, was about two, and the oldest was a sweet little girl, about four. Her big brown eyes, her pigtails, and her smile reminded me of Zsuzsa, my goddaughter back home. I reached out to sit her on my lap and she sleepily snuggled close, resting her head on my chest. The father, Sándor, a tall, handsome, muscular man with dark wavy hair, and a short mustache, was a skilled mechanic in a Csepel motorcycle manufacturing company, and his pretty wife, Kati, worked nearby in the office.

Throwing caution to the wind, they told us that Sándor, despite having been a Communist Party member for years, had become very active in one of the worker's councils, which had sprung up in his factory after October 23, and also had participated in the fighting following the Russian invasion. He knew he was a marked man. He knew he had to leave.

We listened to their story in amazement. Csepel was a sprawling industrial suburb of Budapest, and the Csepel workers were the darlings of the communist regime. They were the embodiment of the proletariat that was used as an example in Marxist-Leninist propaganda to justify communist ideology. Yet here was Sándor, one of those workers, who at the first available opportunity rejected and abandoned the very system that had been supposedly created and maintained for his benefit. Furthermore, if that wasn't bad enough from the communists' point of view, at the same time, he was also eagerly embracing the promise of democracy at great peril to himself and his family.

Seeing the desperation that prompted them to take a chance on a dangerous flight with three small children, we decided to let them join us and we pledged them our help. The spontaneous alliance we formed on the spot was not unlike the ones that were formed around the country during the course of the revolution: a factory worker, an office worker, a technician, and some students, combining their resources for a common goal.

My memory is hazy as to the exact circumstances that followed and the names of the towns and villages we traveled through. I wish I had written an account of these events soon after they occurred, but since I didn't, I have to be content with a reconstruction that might not be accurate in its details.

Rezsö had a map of western Hungary, so we were able to follow the train's progress as we read the station names passing by. Szöny, Ács, Raab, this last one being, we estimated, about half way to Sopron. Our excitement began to mount. We knew it was approximately a day's journey from Budapest to the border, although we were hoping to get to the town of Sopron before sundown. Rezsö's father had done a lot of orienteering in his younger days, so we had a compass and a detailed map of the border area where we were heading, but we had no idea how we would proceed once we reached the town of Sopron. Our hope was that eventually we would end up in, or near, the Austrian town of Wiener-Neustadt. The only fact we knew, or thought we knew, was that we had to find some kind of shelter before dark because of the curfew that was in effect in the three-kilometer-wide so-called protected border zone.

After a while, Pista became restless and disappeared to explore the rest of the train. About an hour later, when he showed up again, obviously pleased with himself, he was full of stories concerning conditions near the border. Despite the curfew, he had learned, the only time it was safe to be outdoors in the countryside was during the night. During the day, both the Hungarian border guards and Russian forces patrolled the fields, confiscating identity cards and arresting people heading for the border.

Looking around, I had to smile to myself. It certainly wasn't difficult for anybody to distinguish the few locals in their embroidered native finery and carrying baskets returning home from Budapest from the numerous city folks trying to escape from the capital, in their best, warmest, city outfits and carrying their backpacks.

Rumor had it, though, that most units on patrol were willing to look the other way if the refugees had money and watches to give to them in exchange for safe passage. We had already heard that back in Budapest and had come prepared. My parents had parted with their watches, as had Rezsö's mother and brother, as well as considerable amounts of money each family member had hidden around the house for emergencies. We also had our own watches on our wrists, should we need them. Nothing we had was expensive or particularly valuable, but reportedly most of the Russians did not seem to know the difference. I noted to myself, with relief, that we all had at our disposal both money and watches, and even if they took everything it was a small price to pay for our lives.

Further good news, according to the stories, was that on the Austrian side of the border, people wanting to help the refugees were lighting campfires and shooting flares into the night sky in order to guide them.

The train seemed to travel slowly, and time seemed to pass even slower. Looking out the window, I noticed that it was a clear, sunny, though cold, and blustery, winter day. I was glad I had dressed warmly, with several layers of clothes under my winter coat, ready for the cold nights in the open. Around noon, we ate the lunches that we had brought with us, and I shared Auntie Mariska's cookies with the others, to the delight of the little girl, Orsi. Oblivious to the dangers around her, she happily chatted with everybody, helping us pass the time. After lunch she and the other two children fell asleep. Kati, her mother was delighted, "It is less difficult to keep a rested child quiet than a tired, cranky one," she explained. Just as we were getting close to the end of our rail journey, I dozed off for a few minutes as well with my head on Rezsö's shoulder.

Around four o'clock, as we neared our destination, the conductor came around to warn people that because there was a contingent of secret police waiting for the train at the next village the engineer had been ordered to make an unscheduled stop at that station. The conductor advised us that the train would slow to a crawl for a few minutes and that if we didn't want to have to explain to those officers our presence in the restricted border area we should jump off. He casually mentioned the name of the closest Austrian village, about twenty kilometers away, and pointed out the direction.

One by one, we jumped, many of us with backpacks on our shoulders. People ran alongside the train to help others and to catch children as their parents dropped them into waiting arms before they themselves jumped. Men jumped first, then small children were dropped and older children jumped on their own, then the mothers followed, then elderly people, and finally young women and girls like me.

Our group had worked out a plan. Rezsö jumped first, followed closely by Feri and Sándor. Next, Kati threw her six-month old infant boy in his bunting from the moving train into

Rezsö's arms. She quickly took the toddler from Pista and threw him to Sándor, who handed him over to Feri. Still on the train, Pista quickly got out of my way to make room for me to hand little Orsi to Kati standing on the steps. "Wheee," Kati called out, smiling at her child encouragingly as she dropped her into her father's outstretched arms, and the little girl squealed in delight. "This is surreal," Kati said before she jumped. Recovering quickly, she took her baby boy from Rezsö, freeing him to assist me, as I prepared to jump from the train, while Pista waited impatiently behind me.

"Don't look down before you leap," those running along the tracks kept saying, "look up, look at me! Don't look down! On your mark, get set, go!" Over and over those on the ground repeated these words to assist those still on the train.

Before I jumped, I did happen to look down, and I immediately understood the wisdom in the advice. Even though the train was traveling slowly, the wooden railroad ties seemed to be passing by underneath my feet with dizzying speed, and the thousands of stones lining the embankment between them looked menacing. Nevertheless, taking a deep breath, I jumped and landed in Rezsö's strong arms, safe and sound.

Stepping back, I looked up and saw an amazing sight, one that I will never forget. As the train, made up of eight cars, a powerful shiny black steam engine up front and a dirty, old, red caboose at the end, was slowly crawling around a curve, at least a hundred people ran alongside it, then away from it, trying to blend into the countryside. As I stood there, I could not help wondering how many of them would have the good fortune to reach their destination. I prayed that we would be among those who did.

The coaches must have been nearly empty when the secret police boarded them at the next station. I hoped they would not realize the complicity of the conductors and the engineer in slowing the train and warning the passengers.

We quickly regrouped, and while the majority of the people followed a path parallel to the railroad tracks in a northwesterly direction, our little party made up of Rezsö, myself, Feri, Pista, and the young family from Csepel, turned away from the railroad tracks and headed to the southwest.

We must have traveled about ten kilometers across the frozen fields when we spotted a couple of soldiers with machine guns on border patrol, marching single file in the distance towards the northeast. We quickly hid in the bushes and waited for at least an hour, lying on the ground, shivering, until they were completely out of sight. The baby was given a piece of bread soaked in wine to keep him quiet, and the other two children enough cough medicine to keep them drowsy. Once we felt safe enough to continue our journey, we took turns carrying them.

We were less fortunate an hour later, when we ran right into a five-man Russian patrol, riding in an open vehicle, guns drawn. Our high school and college Russian language skills served us well then, as we told them that we were on our way to visit our aunt who lived nearby. "*Da, da,*" nodded the platoon leader knowingly, while his men just stood there smiling. We could tell they had heard the story before, and we realized that we could negotiate a price for our safe passage. Transaction completed, the soldiers continued on their way without arresting us, although they did tell us to turn around and head northeast, where the town of Sopron and our aunt were located. We did as they told us. They never looked back to check if we obeyed the order, and I don't think they cared. I believe they were more concerned about counting their loot for the day in the safety of their warm barracks. As soon as the soldiers were out of sight, we doubled back again and continued walking southwest toward what we thought was Austria.

It was getting dark by the time we happened on a small farmhouse. White smoke drifting from the chimney against the setting sun signaled the fact that the occupants were home. They must have seen us approach, for as we drew near, the door opened revealing a handsome elderly couple with warm smiles. The farmer, János, and his wife, Marika, seemed sympathetic to our cause and quickly brought us into their home, carefully looking around to ascertain that nobody saw us. There was no need for explanations. They knew where we had come from and where we were going. It was easy to tell we were not the first refugees they had encountered. They were hungry for news from Budapest, so we informed them of events of the past few days in the capital, while they voiced their concern about their son, who had been conscripted into the army and was stationed near the Polish border.

"I did not raise my son to shoot at his own countrymen," Marika lamented. "I am convinced that he would refuse such an order." She turned her attention to the stove to hide her tears. We assured her that her son must be safe because we heard that the government had ordered all Hungarian army personnel to their barracks, not trusting them to fight for the restoration of the Russian-backed communist regime. What we didn't tell them was the fact that most of those soldiers chose not to return, but had been participating in the fighting against the Russian forces.

Although the farm couple agreed to assist us to get to the border without any remuneration, we insisted that they take most of our *forints*, especially since we knew that the Hungarian currency was practically worthless in Austria. Each of us had the equivalent of about a month's salary, a considerable amount by Hungarian standards. "You must be hungry," Marika observed, as she offered us a tasty supper of *ujházi tyúkleves*, hot chicken soup with vegetables and noodles, with slices of delicious home-baked crusty bread on the side, then *túróscsusza*, pasta with cottage cheese, sour cream and fried bacon bits. We gratefully accepted and ate heartily in the kitchen at a large wooden table next to the warm stove. We topped off our feast with a cup of hot chocolate milk.

After supper, the farmer hid us in the back of a large barn behind the house. According to his plan, we were to stay there till after midnight, when he was going to guide us for the two-hour hike to the border. Being a light sleeper, Rezsö was wide awake and promised to keep watch. Feri and Pista could not sleep, either. They were petrified that the couple was going to betray our little group, despite assurances to the contrary from the rest of us. "We should make a run for it while we can, instead of sitting around," they urged anybody who would listen, but everybody, even Elsie the cow, ignored them. Finally Rezsö told them to shut up or get going by themselves, and they gave up and quieted down. Everything seemed peaceful to me, and events seemed to be unfolding according to plan. Sándor, Kati, and the three children huddled together in an empty stall next to mine, and in no time they had drifted off to sleep. I felt completely exhausted and I fell into a deep sleep as soon as my head hit the hay in a stall right next to Elsie the cow and her calf. I didn't awaken until it was time to leave.

Personally, I never doubted the honesty and good will of the couple. They appeared to be patriotic Hungarians, eager to help their city cousins in their time of need. I placed my trust in them completely.

But sure enough, later that night we heard the footsteps of a night patrol of Hungarian border guards as they showed up at the doorstep of the farmhouse. "We have not seen any strangers lurking around," we heard János tell them, while his wife Marika stood by, most likely nodding in agreement. By then, the couple had washed all the dishes and carefully cleaned the kitchen after us. It was spotless, János told us later. He gave the soldiers several shot glasses of *pálinka,* a strong Hungarian alcoholic beverage, while they stood chatting around the hot kitchen stove, complaining about the weather. Having warmed themselves inside and out, the patrol got ready to leave. János and Marika wished them a safe journey and waved them on their way, watching them depart into the night with their search lamps, and carefully observing till the last one had disappeared over the horizon.

This scene probably repeated itself time and time again at farmhouses along the border. If the guards suspected anything, they most likely turned a blind eye to what they must have seen many times. Unlike the few truly dangerous and vicious members of the elite AVO secret police, who cared only about maintaining their power and privileges, these border patrols did not want Hungarian blood on their hands or consciences. The despised AVO special units were known for taking identity cards in order to later arrest refugees, and for shooting on sight, even women and children. "How fortunate we are," I whispered to Rezsö, "to have come this far." We prayed together for God's protection during the remainder of our journey.

The night was beautiful and clear when we started off on what we hoped would be the last leg of our journey. We silently followed the farmer into the cold, moonlit night, fighting the wind every step of the way as it swirled around us. We were quiet, immersed in private thoughts, as we concentrated on negotiating the frozen, uneven ground under our feet. Before our departure, Sándor and Kati had given all three children the tranquilizers prescribed by their pediatrician back in Budapest to make sure they wouldn't make a noise that would give our party away. This time Kati carried the baby, while the guys took turns carrying the other two. Their unconscious little bodies seemed much heavier. At one point, Kati whispered to me jokingly, "Do you think we have reached Budapest already?" I had to chuckle. Apparently I wasn't the only one who seemed to feel that we have been walking around forever in circles, getting nowhere.

Suddenly, just ahead of us, we saw them: the bonfires and the welcoming flares of Austria. While the bonfires provided a steady glow in the distance, the flares lit up the night sky periodically, pointing the way to freedom. Our guide stopped to say good-bye, shaking our hands as he wished us good luck. After we thanked him for his help, he quickly turned around and walked back towards his home, his family, his fields, and his livestock, deep in his beloved Hungary.

As I was watching him leave, however, I was overcome with a sense of uneasiness. I became acutely aware of the fact that I was leaving my homeland, perhaps forever. I had been raised to be proud of my rich Hungarian heritage, and I treasured Hungarian food, literature, art, music, and history. I was struggling with mixed emotions. On the one hand, I experienced the strong pull of my native land, and guilt over leaving it, but on the other, I felt a sense of elation about my future life in freedom.

"We better keep on moving, and fast." Rezsö urged me. This was no time to be paralyzed by indecision. In the distance, to our left, I could see the outline of a guard tower blocking a portion of the sky, while ahead we could observe a strip of land, devoid of any vegetation, that extended to our left and right. Immediately it dawned on me that this must be part of the minefields, still inside Hungary, one of the many that had been recently cleared. None of us dared to voice our concern about the consequences of stepping on a mine accidentally left behind, although I am sure we all considered the possibility. I took a deep breath and forged ahead with my companions, running across the smooth, frozen ground, single file, till we reached some bushes along the side of a ditch parallel to the strip of land. We helped each other descend the steep embankment, and through the difficult climb up the other side, pushing and pulling as we struggled along. There was no trace of the barbed wire fence, the so-called iron curtain, either. Apparently the posts and the wires had been removed during the summer along with the mines. Tears were running down my face; partly from the cold, partly from sadness, yes, but mostly from relief, as we continued to walk hurriedly further west across what we believed to be a no man's land towards the bright bonfires that were certainly Austria.

Within minutes, people appeared from the darkness, cheerfully greeting us with German accented, *Isten hozta*. Never had we felt so welcome.

It was only then that we knew for certain that we had crossed the border, that we were safe inside Austria.

Chapter Nine

IN AUSTRIA

It was around four o'clock in the morning of December 1, 1956, when we finally felt sure that we had crossed the border into Austria. As soon as we crossed, Austrian, Italian, German, and English volunteers welcomed us with open arms and open hearts. They had braved the elements in the fields near the border, waiting near campfires with thermoses full of hot chocolate and hot tea and warm blankets, to warm both the insides and the outsides of refugees like us.

"*Danke schöne*," we kept repeating, to which the Austrians, smiling, replied in Hungarian, "*szivesen*", "you are welcome." Every one in our group was exhausted and cold. I was chilled to my bones, shivering uncontrollably, and I gratefully accepted the hot drink, wrapping my fingers around the mug, feeling the heat through my gloved hand and also being comforted by the warm liquid's journey through my body to my stomach. The volunteers treated us like heroes, even as we looked to them as saviors. That was the first of many occasions when I marveled at the generosity of the Austrian people who so unselfishly opened their borders and their hearts, instantly turning their country into a second home for thousands of Hungarian fugitives.

We were soon led to the basement of the village's Catholic church, another four kilometers inside the Austrian border, where the locals had decorated the huge hall with paintings and Hungarian folk art and set up cots. There must have been close to a hundred cots there, most of them occupied, as refugees had been arriving throughout the night. In a dining area next to a kitchen there was warm, homemade food: plenty of hot chicken soup, home-baked cookies, and oranges, bananas, and chocolate—delicacies that we ordinary people in communist Hungary had never seen. When we had planned our escape, we had been prepared to go hungry for days, if necessary; instead, to our amazement, we had landed in the midst of plenty.

When I left Budapest, I thought I was adequately dressed for a winter's journey, but apparently my clothing wasn't sufficient for the extremely cold weather. My whole body felt frozen to the point where I was feeling pain instead of cold. Even though the shelter was well heated, it took a long, long time before I stopped shivering.

At the front of the hall several desks were set up where official-looking men interviewed and processed the refugees, recording data and taking coded messages to be broadcast over the airwaves to relatives back in Hungary, glued to their radios and waiting for news. I quickly filled out the form required to send our message: "Blue bird resumed her search for blue eagle." In my mind's eye, I could see my mother and father, Auntie Mariska, and Rezsö's parents and his brother, all rejoicing when they heard our message in the midst of the continuous stream of similar messages. My heart ached for my parents, and I wished they could have been with us, but my mother, with her serious heart condition could not have survived an escape attempt coupled with the uncertainties of having to start a new life from scratch. I silently resolved to at least do my best, however I could, and help make their lives better in Budapest.

Sándor, Kati, and their three children were immediately taken to a hospital, to have the children checked by doctors. The volunteers insisted that this was necessary because of the tranquilizers the children were given during the journey. "Sadly," they explained, "there had been occasions when children did not wake up because of an unintentional overdose or an unexpected reaction to the sedatives." Although our friends' children looked fine, everybody wanted to make sure that indeed they were well and had suffered no ill effects. We said good-bye to them, promising to keep in touch, a promise we were unfortunately not able to keep. Feri and Pista had gotten separated from our group earlier, so now there were only the two of us, Rezsö and I, facing a strange new world together. I looked around the hall. "What an important moment," I thought, as I headed hand-in-hand with my future husband toward a desk for our first interview in the West.

Although there were interpreters, I was eager to start practicing my foreign language skills, so when our interviewer asked, *"Sprechen sie Deutch?"* meaning, "Do you speak German," I replied *"Ya."* I understood most of the questions he posed. However, when I tried to respond in German, I couldn't find the words. Then I switched to English, hoping to do better. I was elated when the man seemed to follow what I was saying in my heavily-accented, halting way and did not call for an interpreter. I silently thanked God for giving me the incentive to start learning these languages, despite the hassles involved in doing it in secret, and Auntie Mici, my teacher, for her guidance and encouragement.

The cheery, bespectacled, middle-aged man who interviewed us seemed touched by our circumstances. "The first, most important step we need to take is for Rezsö and me to get married," I explained. I told him about my promise to Elsa Mama, Rezsö's mother, that we were going to get married by a Catholic priest, in a Catholic Church, by Christmas, if possible. "As to what country we would like to go to, we ask to be sent to the United States, if possible, so I can be reunited with my twin brother, who I believe is heading there. Our second choice," I informed him, "is Canada, where I have a distant cousin living in Montreal. We don't want to stay in Europe. We want to get as far away from the Russians as we possibly can. Putting an ocean between them and us, as soon as possible, seems like an excellent idea." The interviewer assured us that a wedding could be arranged once we reached one of the refugee camps. "I am sure you will reach one of your desired destinations," he reassured us smiling. I am sure he had heard similar sentiments expressed by other refugees.

After the interview, Rezsö and I settled down with our blankets on adjacent cots, excitedly discussing the events of the previous day. It was morning now, and the sun shone down on us through a small window near the ceiling. We were waiting to be sent to one of the refugee camps further inside Austria when three young, prosperous-looking gentlemen approached us. It turned out that they were visiting the area to assess the needs of the Hungarian refugees. The men belonged to the Maltese Cross Society, a Catholic charitable organization, one of many religious groups that came to the aid of refugees after the Soviet invasion. The three men sat down on our cots with us and struck up a conversation in English. They wanted to know about our relationship, our backgrounds, our professions, and our activities during the revolution. They asked many questions, listened intently, and took notes as I responded or translated Rezsö's remarks. With my halting English, I stumbled along well enough to provide an accurate picture of our past and was able to adequately describe our dreams for the future. They seemed satisfied with the conversation, and soon they smiled and said good-bye, wishing us good luck.

To our astonishment, the trio returned in about an hour, and Kurt S, their spokesman, proceeded to outline a proposal they had for us. He offered to take us to Vienna in his car and promised sponsorship by the society during our stay in Austria. Their generous offer included housing and a church wedding, if we were sure that that was what we truly wanted. We could not believe our good luck and gratefully accepted his invitation.

Riding in the warm Volkswagen toward Vienna was immensely preferable to the journey we had taken in the poorly - heated train across the drab Hungarian countryside just the day before. Today's journey felt luxurious, and Vienna seemed magical as its ornate buildings glistened in the early morning sunlight.

For a couple of days we stayed at Kurt's apartment in Vienna, trying to register at different refugee agencies, the most prominent one being the International Rescue Committee, for meal tickets, toiletries, and clothing. We acquired a "gray card," which identified us as legal refugees and allowed us free travel on the buses and tramways of Vienna. The registration process also took care of our social needs. As we waited in line after line with other freshly arrived refugees, we were able to keep up with developments in Hungary. We asked questions, trying to find my brother and Rezsö's friend, Iván, or any other acquaintance, but to no avail.

Kurt had a small apartment, but because he was a bachelor, it was not considered appropriate for me to stay there. Luckily, friends of his, a young man and his wife, offered to house us in their spacious home. Hans and Helga O. were both lawyers, who, in anticipation of starting a family, had a large apartment close to the center of Vienna. They could not have been kinder to us if we had been their own flesh and blood.

Unfortunately, no sooner were we settled there, than I came down with a terrible cold that developed into pneumonia, probably a consequence of the long, cold journey in the open fields. We should have been standing in line at the United States and Canadian embassies to be registered as prospective immigrants, but, instead, there I was, lying in bed with a high temperature and horrendous headaches, sleeping for days. I was not able to move.

I kept begging Rezsö to go by himself and register us at the United States and Canadian embassies, but he refused to go without me. He said he didn't want to leave me alone while I was sick. I was (and still am) convinced that since he didn't like crowds and because he was impatient with the endless waiting and felt insecure by himself, he had decided it was easier to wait for me. I was worried, frustrated, and resentful about his stubborn refusal to act on his own. I could not help thinking that had the tables been turned, had he been the sick one, not only would I have taken care of him, but I would also have gone by myself to take care of the important business affecting our future well-being.

In the meantime, unbeknownst to us, my brother, Johnny, was already on his way to the United States. While waiting in line at the embassy in Vienna, he heard a rumor that the Americans had opened a temporary office to process refugees in Salzburg. Figuring that traveling three hours in a warm bus was immensely preferable to waiting in line on the cold streets of Vienna, he had decided to take a chance and check it out. Once there, Johnny was able to walk in and register without waiting. He got accepted in two days and within a week found himself on a four-engine, turboprop charter plane heading for McGuire Air Force Base in New Jersey. On December 11, he was walking the streets of New York City, taking in the sights.

All over the country, ordinary Americans and institutions had responded generously to the plight of the Hungarian refugees arriving at their shores. Upon his arrival, Johnny managed, through an interpreter, to convey to the interviewing officer his burning desire to study electrical engineering. The officer must have seen a spark, for despite Johnny's complete lack of English language skills, he presented Johnny with the University of Mississippi's full scholarship offer to a Hungarian refugee to study electrical engineering. My brother gratefully seized the opportunity without hesitation. What a wonderful difference that long-term partnership between Johnny and the university made in the lives of countless people over the years! His generous contributions funded endowments and supported the engineering school and many deserving students.

Meanwhile, back in Vienna, lying in bed, sick and helpless, I was getting extremely frustrated. In addition to worrying about our prospects for reaching North America, I was also petrified that the Russians would use the Hungarian refugees as a pretext to invade neutral little Austria before we had a chance to leave. I was afraid that Russia would be emboldened by the fact that, despite the rhetoric, the West had not provided military support for our revolution. I was afraid that, after all we had endured, I still might end up in Siberia instead of New York or Montreal.

Although my worst fears did not materialize, it did turn out that our delay in registering in a timely manner cost us admittance to the United States. The government closed the Hungarian Immigration quota before our names came up on the list, and there was no firm commitment to the people who were left behind. The delay also cost us months of waiting for our turn to get into Canada.

Once I got better, and we finally took care of registering at the two embassies, the long waiting game began. Other than checking the progress of our case every day, there was not much else we could do. At different relief agencies, we registered the names and addresses of friends and relatives back home in Hungary so that aid packages of food and clothing could be delivered to those still in Budapest. There were long lines everywhere. Standing in lines, waiting for our turn, occupied us most of the day. But we didn't mind, for it felt good to be able to do something for those we had left behind. It eased our guilt about abandoning family and friends.

With plenty of time on our hands, we embarked on a journey of discovery in the beautiful historical city of Vienna. Because cultural agencies donated free passes to Hungarian refugees, getting to know the city became an affordable, most pleasant pastime. Over the centuries, Vienna had provided an excellent setting for outstanding cultural and scientific achievements in the fields of art, literature, music, medicine, and architecture, all of which was reflected in the magnificent baroque and Gothic castles, churches, museums, theaters, statues, and buildings. We spent days exploring Vienna's most famous landmark, St Stephen's Cathedral, which dated back to the twelfth century. This cathedral is one of Europe's most important examples of Gothic architecture, and its naves are filled with masterpieces of painting and sculpture. We also spent days touring Schönbrunn Palace, where we marveled at the grand ballroom, the Gobelin Room with its tapestries and ornate furniture, the Palace Theatre, the Zoological Garden, and the beautifully maintained grounds with their fountains. We visited the bronze statue of Johann Strauss, the "Waltz King," and listened to his famous "Blue Danube" and other waltzes on Saturday afternoons at the nearby "Kursalon" in the city park. The Viennese embraced us when we became homeless. We never forgot their generosity. Our appreciation and love for them has lasted a lifetime.

We still had some Hungarian money left over from our trip, which we exchanged at an exorbitant rate into Austrian shillings. We also had a few American dollars that Rezsö's father had saved up illegally over the years and given to us when we left.

Using some of our shillings, we bought a small English-Hungarian-English dictionary, a beginner's English textbook, and two small copybooks in a second-hand bookstore. That was when Rezsö, in his slow, thorough, methodical way, started to learn English. Since I had the rudiments of the grammar pretty well mastered already, I was able to help him, while I concentrated on expanding my own vocabulary and tried to continue my studies at my level. Each day, we diligently spent an hour in the morning and an hour in the afternoon on our lessons, while I also grabbed every opportunity I could find to practice speaking English. Luckily, Kurt, and our hosts, Hans and Helga, spoke English well, so we were able to communicate with them. These generous people helped us in so many ways that we can never hope to repay our debt to them.

Meanwhile, Kurt and his friends were making plans for our wedding. They helped us with the necessary paperwork, arranged for the civil nuptials at City Hall (the *Rathaus*) on December 21 and for the church wedding with a Hungarian priest on December 26 at Saint Stephan's Kirche.

It was decided that for the civil ceremony I was to wear my light gray pleated wool skirt and white, shirt-blouse, while Rezsö would wear his gray suit, shirt and tie. This was appropriate, for these garments were part of the outfits we wore when we escaped from Hungary. To me, they represented the continuity of our lives.

For the church wedding, our Austrian friends helped me choose a simple, royal blue, light wool outfit in a department store; it was similar to my high school graduation dress. One of the mothers made a pink Hungarian-style headpiece with a short, pink veil. Somebody lent me a pearl necklace with matching clip-on earrings, and somebody else, a fur coat. I felt like a princess.

Using our American dollars, we shopped for wedding bands and, although I would have gotten married with a rubber band, to my delight we were able to find a jeweler who sold us two thin fourteen-karat gold wedding bands for the money we had available. That was the combined engagement and wedding ring I wore for the next thirty-three years of my life.

The morning of the civil ceremony passed uneventfully. It was a gray, cloudy day. We arrived at the appointed time at City Hall with our Austrian witnesses, went through the short ceremony, signed the books, and accepted congratulations from the judge who officiated.

In the afternoon, we met with the Hungarian priest at the church. He was a balding, middle-aged man with a warm personality, a refugee himself, who had been imprisoned in

Hungary by the communists, along with Cardinal Mindszenty, the prelate of the Hungarian Catholic Church. As he shook hands with us, I noticed that parts of his fingers were missing at different joints on both of his hands. This was the first time I had ever met someone who had been tortured by the dreaded Hungarian secret police. I had to fight the physical pain that enveloped me, though it lodged itself in my head and triggered a vicious migraine attack later that night.

The Father talked to us about God, the church, and about the sanctity of marriage. I think he realized that although chronologically we were still very young—I was nineteen and Rezsö twenty-two—because of our life experiences, we both were mature well beyond our years. He tried to convince me of the practicality of converting to the Catholic faith, but despite my familiarity with the religion, for some unknown reason, I did not feel comfortable doing it at that time—to my later regret, for that would have simplified my life in many ways. I reassured him, however, that true to my pledge to Elsa Mama, I was going to support my husband in practicing his religion and that I would raise our children in the Catholic faith. He seemed satisfied and agreed to perform the wedding ceremony that would make us man and wife in the eyes of God and the Catholic Church.

We had Christmas Eve dinner with Hans and Helga O., then went to a beautiful midnight Mass in a small, old Catholic church located on a narrow street. Even though I was not familiar with most of the hymns, I was able to join in with some of the Christmas carols, like "Silent Night" and "Oh, Tannenbaum," in Hungarian, of course. My heart sang, whether I knew the carols or not. What relief I felt as I began to realize that we didn't have to worry about who would see us, who would hear us, and the consequences if anybody did see or hear us. We were free.

Chapter Ten

TASTING FREEDOM

On Christmas morning, we succeeded in telephoning Rezsö's parents for a few minutes. They promised to visit my parents, who did not have a telephone, to pass on all the good news about us. Elsa Mama was especially pleased that we were going to be married in a Catholic church by a Hungarian Catholic priest, and she promised to visit her church at the same time as our wedding to pray for us. We mailed Christmas cards to our parents to show we were thinking of them, hoping that eventually the cards would be delivered.

In the afternoon, we were invited to the group's sumptuous dinner party at the beautiful home of Kurt's mother. What struck me was how happy and carefree everybody was, and how eager everybody seemed to include us as equals. As a combined Christmas and wedding present, all the invited guests gave us clothing and some money. I noted with irony that I had more possessions after living for three weeks in Vienna than I had had after almost three years of working in Budapest. If only my parents could see me now, I kept thinking.

The most exciting present for me, though, was a pair of tickets to Richard Wagner's *Tristan and Isolde* at the Vienna State Opera House *(Staatsoper)* for a January performance. To hear Wagner in Vienna was a dream that even I, the self-proclaimed queen of dreamers, had never ever dared to dream. The furthest I had gotten before was debating with Rezsö the possibility of buying standing room tickets to a matinee presentation before we were to leave for North America. To receive orchestra seats to an evening of grand opera brought tears to my eyes.

After the party the night before our wedding, Rezsö went to stay with Kurt in his apartment, while I went home with Hans and Helga for my last night as a single girl. I had a hard time falling asleep. I took stock of my past, its joys and hardships, and looked forward to the new life that was about to begin. I thanked God for being alive despite the many disasters that could have ended my life; beginning with my small weight at birth, then the Nazis, the war, and last, but not least, the Russians. I wondered to what end God had spared me. Not finding an answer that night, I resolved to search for His plan for me and to earn my keep on this earth, to make my life count professionally and privately, and to be the best wife, the best mother, the best Julie I could possibly be.

The next day, on December 26, I took a taxi with Hans and Helga to the church, arriving about fifteen minutes ahead of the appointed time of three o'clock in the afternoon. To my great surprise Rezsö was already there, waiting for me, handsome as ever, his blonde hair contrasting against the borrowed dark suit on his broad shoulders. During our courtship, he had been chronically late all the time, driving me crazy with his tardiness. I used to tease him that he would be late for his own wedding, miss the ceremony, and have to stay a bachelor for the rest of his life. I spotted him standing in the small vestibule, grinning at me, as soon as I walked in. "I can't believe you got here before me!" I said. "I bet Kurt made sure you were not late." "Kurt had nothing to do with my early arrival," he retorted. "I did it all by myself, just to prove your predictions wrong." I just smiled, for we both knew better.

The ceremony was held in a small, ornate, side chapel in the historic Saint Stephan's Kirche in the center of Vienna, where Austrian monarchs like Maria Teresa and Franz Joseph had been wed. Kurt was the best man, and Helga was my matron of honor. As I walked down the isle with Hans, standing in for my father, I noticed that the old wooden pews were filled with smiling strangers. Members of the society and their friends had turned out in support, embracing the two homeless young people embarking on a new life without their families. Floating along to the strains of the gorgeous wedding march, I smiled back, while tears of gratitude swelled in my eyes behind the pink veil. I was deeply moved as we knelt at the altar and promised "to love, cherish and honor each other for better or for worse, in sickness and in health, until death do us part." At that time, I still believed in fairy tales, where all the princesses lived happily ever after, loved, cherished, and protected by their princes. As we were driven off to our honeymoon, I was truly happy in the firm belief that all my troubles were finally over. Now I had a partner for life who loved, cherished, and honored me "till death do us part." It was fortunate that it never occurred to me at that moment that real life does not always live up to fairy tale promises.

Another special present, which came from an anonymous donor, was a three-day honeymoon trip to a nearby mountain resort in the Alps. After the wedding, Hans L., another friend of Kurt's, who was one of the witnesses at our civil wedding ceremony, picked us up in his small yellow Volkswagen bug and drove us to a modest hotel in a valley that looked exactly like a picture perfect scene in a travel brochure. Neither of us had ever skied before, and we didn't have the required clothing, so we were content just to watch as people glided gracefully around us. We were able to rent skates to go skating outdoors, however, and we sashayed around hand-in-hand to the strains of Strauss waltzes. The mountain air was invigorating, the weather was sunny, and the view was magnificent. We had to keep pinching ourselves to be sure that it was not a dream.

Time marched on. February, March, still no news from the

embassies, and the next couple of months became progressively more difficult. We were eager to get on with our lives, but we were in limbo. We had to wait to be admitted as immigrants. I am sure that Hans and Helga, generous as they were when they first offered their hospitality, did not figure on having us this long, yet they unselfishly insisted on keeping us till we were processed to travel to our future home country. I tried to make myself useful by cleaning and cooking, but we felt increasingly more uncomfortable about invading their privacy and imposing on their good nature.

The days turned into weeks, then into months. We explored the sights of Vienna through the lens of a Voigtlander camera we bought for Rezsö, but of course we used it sparingly to save the expense of film and development. Occasionally we went to see a movie. I'll never forget the first American film we saw in Vienna, *Roman Holiday*. I was completely charmed by this romantic comedy, the beautiful, Audrey Hepburn, the dashingly handsome Gregory Peck, and the delightful Eddie Albert. The film contained no communist propaganda, no socialist double talk. It was just a simple romance between two attractive young people. It was uncomplicated, light, funny, entertaining. I loved every minute of it.

In a letter from my parents we got the news that my brother was doing well with his scholarship at the University of Mississippi as a first year electrical engineering student. I knew it wasn't going to be easy, especially since he couldn't speak a word of English when he left Hungary, but I also knew that he was going to make the most of this chance.

One day, we met Susie, my friend from elementary school, and her boyfriend, Bob, at one of the restaurants that honored food vouchers from the refugees. They were on their way to New York (where she had an aunt) by boat the following week, and they were planning to get married as soon as they arrived. We also bumped into my cousin, Eva, and her boyfriend, Robert, a young mechanical engineer. They were on their way to Australia (where he had relatives), and they were planning to get married there. She was not looking forward to the long sea voyage, but was eager to start her new life in Sydney. She tried to convince us to go to Australia, but that was just a little too far for me, especially since I knew that Johnny was already in the States.

The news from Hungary was depressing. The Russians were consolidating their stronghold on the country, and the dreaded AVO had reestablished their spy network in the schools, offices, and factories. The borders were being closed down. The flood of refugees became a trickle, then by the end of March, the flow practically dried up.

But the most depressing news was personal, and it came in a letter from Gyuri, Rezsö's brother. He informed us that our friend, Robie Bán, had been arrested while fighting at Széna Square, where the revolutionaries had put up their fiercest resistance against the invading Russian forces after November 4. No wonder Rezsö had not been able to reach him the night before we left Budapest. Unbeknownst to his mother, he was already in prison. I was heartbroken over the news and kept praying for a miracle to save him. My prayers went unanswered. Later we learned that he was tried, condemned as a bourgeois counter-revolutionary, and in 1958 put to death by hanging at the same time Imre Nagy, Pál Maléter, and other heroes of the revolution were tried and executed for their "crimes against the state." Cellmates recalled later that Robie accepted his fate without bitterness and went to his death bravely, with his head held high.

Finally, at the end of April, we were notified, that we had been approved for permanent residency in Canada and were to report to a processing camp in preparation for transportation. We were ready. No, we were more than ready. We said goodbye to Vienna and our Austrian friends, promising to keep in touch and return one day. Canada was beckoning, and we answered her call gratefully.

The processing camp was located in an elementary school in a small village. We shared an old classroom equipped with cots and wardrobes for dividers with two other young couples. Although camp life was not nearly as comfortable as Hans and Helga's home, we knew it was temporary, so we didn't mind the nearly three weeks we had to spend there. Most of the time, we were studying English or reading English language books about Canada. The camp had a small library of donated books. Spring had arrived, and crocuses, daffodils, and tulips were blooming.

For Hungarians, it is difficult to learn to read English. That is because, in the Hungarian written language, every word is pronounced phonetically. That is, every vowel with or without an accent, every consonant, alone or in combination with another, has a unique sound, regardless of its position. To learn to read, you just have to learn the sound each letter represents, connect the sounds, and then you can read anything. Because in English each letter can have a different sound, depending on its position, it is very difficult for most people to acquire the skills required for reading English. Seeing the struggles of others, I appreciated how fortunate I was to have had expert instruction for a head start.

I also liked to play with the many children who freely roamed the camp, for which their parents were very appreciative. One day we found a patch of wild forget-me-nots in a nearby field and all the children gathered small bouquets for their parents in the camp. I recalled how my father used to bring bouquets to my mother and me at the first sign of spring. Later, I organized little English classes to teach them essential phrases, such as "My name is _____," "I am lost," and so on. We read nursery rhymes and sang little songs in English. I found a simple Walt Disney songbook in the library, and so we learned to sing, "Whistle while you work" and of course "When you wish upon a star." One morning, sitting by the piano in the library and surrounded by children of all ages, basking in the bright morning sunshine, I found myself singing the song I had learned from Clara in elementary school; "Somewhere over the rainbow, way up high, there's a land that I heard of once in a lullaby. Somewhere over the rainbow, skies are blue, and the dreams that you dare to dream really do come true."

Although Rezsö and I had very few possessions, we were happy. We were optimistic about the future and felt ready for whatever challenges life was going to send our way.

While we were eagerly anticipating our first trip by airplane, many people were afraid to fly and chose to wait for a ship to take them overseas. Not us. We opted for the plane ride. Buffeted by waves on a small ship for two weeks across the Atlantic Ocean was not our idea of adventure, while taking to the air was. Although we had never flown before, we were excited and not the least bit apprehensive. We were told that the plane would stop for refueling in Greenland and that the whole trip was going to take about fourteen hours. We were warned that some of us might get airsick, but I just knew I wasn't going to be among those. I was determined that I was going to enjoy the flight, and so I did, every minute of it.

On May 13, 1957, a chartered four-engine turboprop took off from Swechat Airport in Vienna into the clear, blue sky, headed for Dorval Airport in Montreal, Canada. It was carrying about fifty Hungarian refugees, plus their hopes and dreams. Among those on board was a young couple, Rezsö and Julianna C., looking to the future with confidence, eager to start their new life together.

Chapter Eleven

BEGINNING ANEW

As the plane soared into the blue sky above scattered clouds, leaving both clouds and Europe behind, I knew in my heart with unmistakable certainty that we had made the right decision on that fateful December morning when we started our journey in Budapest, out of the stifling oppression that was about to envelop Hungary again. I was happily and confidently anticipating my new life with my new husband, on a new continent, in my new homeland, where under just laws I could say what I wanted, do what I wanted, and enjoy the fruits of my life's labor in freedom.

I thought about my parents and the sacrifices they had made for us. I could see and hear my father again, checking our homework, exhorting us to study, to work hard, and always do our best. "The key to success in life is education," he would say. "Knowledge is power. The only thing they can't take away from you is what's inside your head," he would repeat to us over and over. "A human being can achieve true, lasting happiness only if he is able to fulfill his own potential," I remembered him saying. "Search for and find the gifts that you have, and share them with your fellow men, for as the Bible says, by giving you will receive. The takers, the parasites of this world might have more material possessions, but they will never know true happiness like those who contribute to the welfare of their fellow human beings and the betterment of society. The world does not owe you a living, neither respect, nor love. You have to earn it." We all respected and loved my father, a wise man who learned his lessons well while attending the prestigious school of hard knocks. He graduated with honors, as attested to by all who knew him.

My thoughts shifted from the past to the future. Although I was hoping to find a job as a draftsman and Rezsö was hoping for a position in engineering, we were willing to accept any honest work in the beginning to earn and save some money. We were young, we had time to build our future, and I was confident in our abilities.

My thoughts leaped ahead, I imagined the children we were going to have and felt an overwhelming wave of love for them envelop me. I rejoiced in the opportunities we would eventually be able to provide for them with a good education. From an early age, I told myself, our children would attend the best schools, have music lessons, take part in art classes, and participate in sports like swimming and skating to enrich their lives. While the plane was flying steadily towards its destination, I happily drifted on the wings of my fantasies until I fell asleep, at peace with the world, resting my head on my husband's broad shoulders. I had what I had always desired: **S**omething to **L**ove, **S**omething to **D**o and **S**omething to **H**ope for.

Epilogue

The rest of my story is waiting to be told in a second memoir. My brother, Johnny, completed his studies in electrical engineering at the University of Mississippi in 1960. In 1971, as a Sloan Executive Fellow, he earned a Master's Degree in Management from Stanford University. For years, he worked for IBM, before becoming one of the cofounders of ADAPTEC, a computer company, eventually becoming its President and CEO. He was recognized by his alma mater with the Distinguished Alumnus, and the Engineer of Distinction Awards. He retired in Florida in 1998, and we keep in touch by telephone and visit each other often.

My parents visited us in Canada and the United States, but they lived out their lives in Hungary. My mother spent her last few years bedridden and died of heart failure on her fifty-fourth birthday. My father lived to be a relatively healthy seventy-eight years old and died in his sleep.

Auntie Mariska suffered a heart attack in 1961, and died at home shortly after, surrounded by her adopted family and her friends.

After my children were grown, I visited Budapest many times, in both private and professional capacities. I have kept in touch with my cousin, Zita, my brother-in-law, Gyuri, and other friends and former classmates. It is worth mentioning that Aunt Ika is still going strong at ninety-four, living a remarkably independent life alone in Budapest.

My cousin, Eva, and her husband, Rob, eventually moved to

Canada from Australia. Rob is a Professor Emeritus of mechanical engineering at the University of Toronto, and Eva had a long career as a design draftsman before her retirement. They have two children, Tom and Peter, as well as two grandchildren.

Robert (Robie) Bán, our friend, is resting now in the Rákoskereszturi Cemetery, in a place of honor established in 1988 for all the martyrs who were executed by the communists with Imre Nagy in June, 1958. He was only twenty-two years old when his life was cut short. We named our eldest son, born in 1962, Robert in his memory.

Susie, my friend from elementary school, and her husband, Bob, live in Milwaukee, where she pursued her career in dressmaking with considerable success. They have two children, Margie and David, and two grandchildren. My friend, Lia, had a short and tragic life in Budapest after a crippling traffic accident. Others coped as best as they could in Hungary, whereas all those who escaped after the revolution in 1956 flourished in the West.

Years ago I heard Gloria Steinem in a television interview say, "Many of us are living out the unlived lives of our mothers, because they were not able to become the unique people they were born to be." My parents were gifted in many ways, yet history denied them opportunities to fully live their lives. They had to struggle to live ordinary lives under extraordinary circumstances. Their legacy lies in the children they protected and raised and in their descendants. I believe that the promise my mother had, I fulfilled. The potential my father had, my brother fulfilled.

With hard work, and fate smiling on Johnny and me, I trust that in our own way we were able to make a difference for the better in the lives of many people, thus validating our parents' struggles to ensure our survival. To their descendants, our children and grandchildren, we pass the torch, leaving a rich legacy on which to build their own lives along the road to the fulfillment of their own destiny.

I still speak English with a slight Hungarian accent; rolling my *r*'s, mangling my *v*'s and *w*'s, accompanied by deep vowels and melodic tones popularized by Zsa Zsa Gábor, a well known Hollywood actress. However, I have been thinking and dreaming in English for decades now (without, I believe, any accent). I like to think that my writing reflects this fact, and that I do not write with an accent either. There is nothing wrong with speaking English in America with an accent. As a matter of fact, I have been told many times that it is refreshing to hear English spoken correctly with an accent. Nevertheless, I believe written language should be near perfect. Throughout the creation of this work, I have striven for perfection, and I apologize if occasionally I have fallen short.

I am a proud American now, I fly our flag from my balcony, sing our anthem, recite the pledge of allegiance, vote, volunteer, and go to church. I treasure my freedom. At the same time, I cherish my past: my Hungarian heritage and my Canadian bonds. It is my fervent hope that one day my descendants will get to know and learn to understand, appreciate, respect, and honor that rich heritage as well. Perhaps reading this memoir will be their first step toward that end.

Julie's parents, Katalin and Zsigmond in 1957

Rezsö's parents, Elsa Mama and Rezsö Senior in 1957

Printed in the United States
1324800003B/103-126